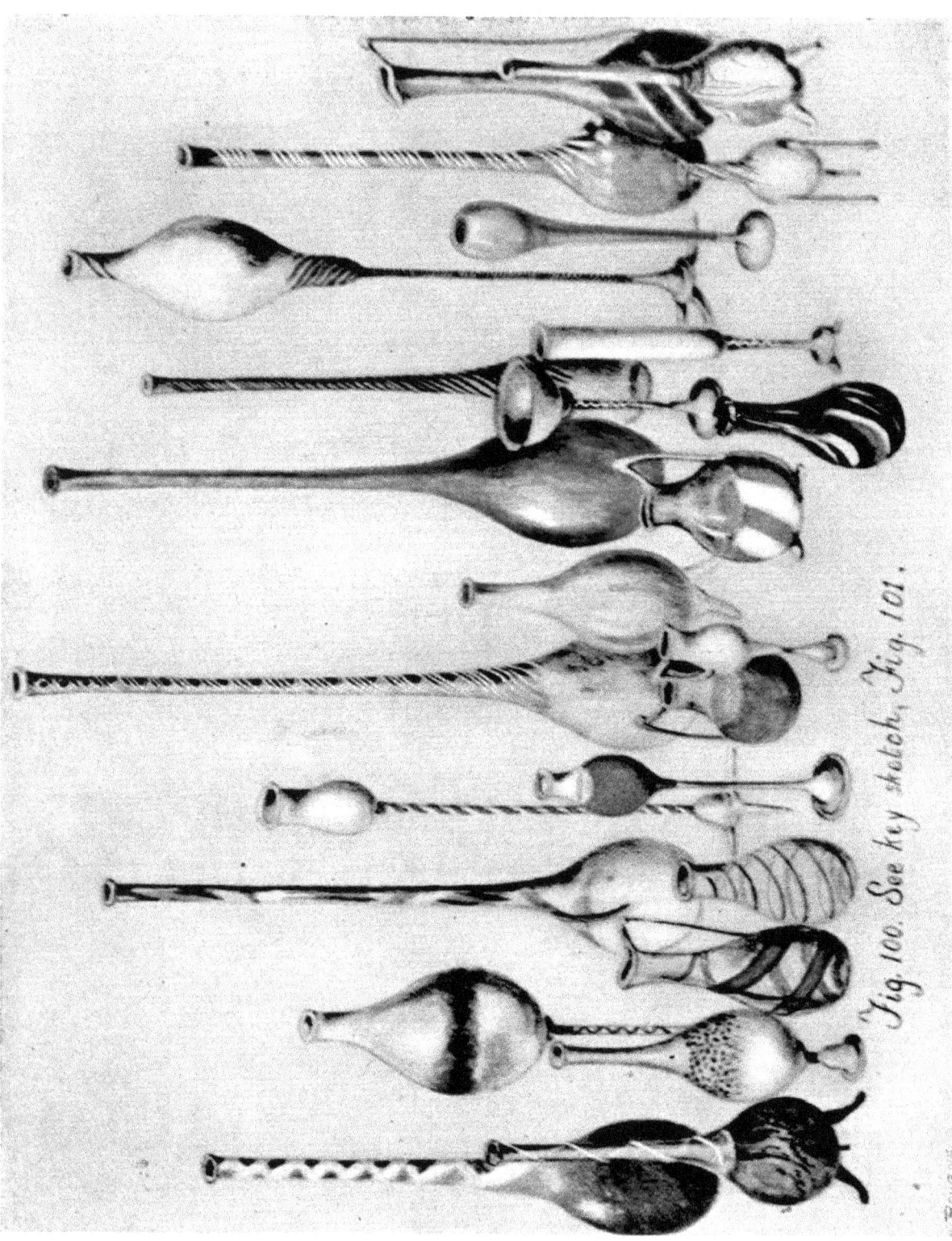

Fig. 100. See key sketch, Fig. 101.

MINIATURE DECORATIVE WORK.
(For details of making, see Chapter IX.)

Three-Color Blocks by
A. BOURNE & CO.,
75 Ludgate Hill, E.C.

(see back cover)

Copyright © 2008 Merchant Books

ISBN 1-60386-101-7

Digitalized by
Watchmaker Publishing
All Rights Reserved

Glass Blowing and Working

For Amateurs, Experimentalists, and Technicians

Based upon a Course of Lecture-Demonstrations given under the Auspices of the Technical Education Committee of the Middlesex County Council.

WITH
Numerous Illustrations

BY
THOMAS BOLAS, F.C.S., F.I.C.

CONTENTS

CHAP.		PAGE
	FRONTISPIECE—COLORED REPRODUCTIONS OF DECORATIVE WORK,	2
I.	GLASS WORK IN MINIATURE AS A DECORATIVE PASTIME, ETC. ETC.,	7
II.	THE BLOWPIPE AND BELLOWS,	20
III.	MINOR TOOLS AND APPLIANCES,	53
IV.	GLASS. RODS AND TUBING—GAUGING—STORING—PRESERVATION—CLEANING,	63
V.	VARIOUS METHODS OF WORKING AND BLOWING GLASS,	78
VI.	EXAMPLES OF SPECIAL ARTICLES FOR LABORATORY AND OTHER USES,	171
VII.	COLORING AND MODIFYING MATERIALS, ETC.,	189
VIII.	AGING, DISINTEGRATION, AND DECAY OF GLASS, ETC. ETC.,	194
IX.	FANCY AND DECORATIVE ARTICLES MADE AT THE BLOWPIPE,	198
X.	GLASS MAKING AT THE BLOWPIPE AND ON A LABORATORY SCALE,	204
XI.	THE BIBLIOGRAPHY OF GLASS,	207
XII.	INDEX,	210
	Recipes For Flint Glass Making	217

PREFACE.

I HAVE aimed at making the present Work not only a laboratory, workshop, or household guide to the various phases of Glass Working at the Blowpipe, but also, to some extent, technically educational in the real sense of the term; as leading towards an understanding why each particular thing is done, and as facilitating that interdrift of method from craft to craft which is so conducive to progress.

THOMAS BOLAS.

LONDON, *January* 1898.

Various methods of working and details hitherto unpublished, besides novel articles, were shown in the author's recent course of lecture demonstrations given under the auspices of the Technical Education Committee of the Middlesex County Council, and are described in the present work. Without wishing to enforce so illiberal a doctrine as the copyright of technical subject-matter itself,—a doctrine which has been upheld in the Law Courts,—the Publishers suggest that the source should be mentioned by those who may gather hitherto unpublished matter from the present book and incorporate it in their writings.

Fig. 1.
Glass Blowers From Kunckeln's Ars Vitraria Experimentalis, 1689.

CHAPTER I.

GLASS-WORKING IN MINIATURE AS A DECORATIVE PASTIME, AS A MEANS OF MANUAL TRAINING, AND AS AN AID IN HUMAN PROGRESS. THE EGYPTIANS AS GLASS-WORKERS. THE ROMAN AND VENETIAN PERIODS. THE NEWER GLASS INDUSTRY.

Decorative Work at Home.—Comparatively few persons realise that it is practicable, and indeed very easy, to make many small glass articles of use and ornament in the most diminutive of private rooms, and this without more extensive or numerous appliances than such as occupy the space of an ordinary sewing machine on its usual treadle stand. Yet 200 years ago (in 1689), Kunckeln called very prominent attention to the facility with which glass may be worked as a kind of home industry. Kunckeln was one of the independent discoverers of the element phosphorus, and, in his later days, he was a chamberlain in the Brandenburg Court, and it was while he held this office that he issued the 1689 edition (I believe there were two earlier editions although I have not seen them) of his *Ars Vitraria Experimentalis*, a small quarto of between four and five hundred pages, containing many illustrations. Opposite to page 399 of this remarkable work is a plate engraving which shows two gentlemen and a lady, in the costume of the time, seated at a glass-blowing table, placed in a domestic apartment. In connection with this matter, he points out that with a few canes of coloured or enamel glass tube or rod, and appliances of the most simple character, the best productions of the glass-houses may be equalled or, indeed, surpassed by the home-worker, although such productions are necessarily on a miniature scale. The quaint engraving is reproduced (fig. 1), and it shows those pear-shaped bellows which are still recognised as the best, although the mounting is somewhat clumsy. The lamp shown is intended for oil, and is a form still in use, although it may often be more conveniently replaced by a gas blowpipe. The hood over the table is intended to carry off the odorous fumes of the partly-burned oil. Kunckeln's work is largely founded on earlier books by Neri and others, and I am unable to say how far I may be attributing to Kunckeln that which should be ascribed to others. It is, however, interesting to note that Kunckeln gives much in his work which comes up from time to time as new, and anticipates several patents of the past thirty years. The book, however, is but little known, in spite of the fact that a French edition appeared in 1752.

The more utilitarian side of glass-working at the lamp or table blowpipe is by no means confined to the production of fancy or ornamental articles, as many prime factors in scientific and industrial progress are thus made. Among these may be mentioned the barometer and the thermometer, both so essential to navigators; the latter, in the shape of the deep-sea thermometer of Negretti and Zambra, having saved many an ocean-going steamer from collision with an iceberg. Among the more recent applications to human service of glass-working at the lamp are the incandescence electric lamp, and the Crookes's high Vacuum tube The latter, when used in conjunction with a photographic plate, has given us a means of searching the inner structure of iron plates as used in shipbuilding, and in locating other matters hitherto closed to human ken.

Educational Aspect.—Another and by no means unimportant aspect of glass-working at the lamp is its educational bearing. As cultivating delicacy of touch and perception it stands almost alone, and in the matter of cultivating immediate and accurate correspondence between the actions of the hand and the perceptions of the eye it has all the merits of cricket, fencing, or pugilism, with the advantage of being suited to those who do not care for such robust means of training themselves. Glass-working stands perhaps by itself as a training for independence of the two hands, or exact correspondence as the case may be. In this respect piano or organ playing may, in some cases, run it somewhat closely, but music for pianists and organists is often constructed or selected especially to suit very right-handed persons, in which case the training value of the exercise becomes less, and, moreover, there are very many who have no inclination to train themselves on the piano or organ. The harmony of action between the two hands of an expert glass-worker is probably beyond everything in technology; as, for example, when a longish tube, unequal in diameter at the two ends, is softened in the middle and then operated on, say by blowing in at one end. Not only must the two hands rotate the piece at the same angular rate while before the blowpipe, but each half must be balanced on the hands. When taken from the flame for blowing, the rotation must be maintained, and both hands must move in such exact correspondence as to put no unintentional strain on the soft part. These actions must not in any way be disturbed by the shifting of the tube to the mouth for blowing; indeed, as a matter of fact, the keeping up of a steady blast with the bellows soon becomes reflex, as also the continual rotation of the piece with similar and simultaneous impulses at each end, even when the diameters of the two ends are unequal.

As training the Perceptions.—The power of quickly appreciating proportion, magnitude, form, weight, strain or temperature must necessarily be cultivated, as in almost every case verification comes after and not before the event, although the glass-blower, like the smith, may contrive simple gauges for use *during* the acts when he has several similar pieces to make. As expertness comes, these are often found to be rather a hindrance. Speaking generally, glass-working is somewhat akin to smithing, as regards its training and intellectual aspects; but smithing, unfortunately, is ill-adapted to be a home occupation, although it now fills a useful place in the curriculum of many schools for boys. There is, however, one generic difference between glass-working and smithing. In the latter the shaping of the softened material is by tools and handicraft, in the former it is mainly by cunningly taking advantage of natural forces, and all through the work the operator has to count on and allow for the various forces which tend to alter the shape of the piece.

First Steps easy.—In spite of the many difficulties and delicacies of the higher glass-blowing, a person of moderate ability may almost immediately make simple articles, and rise gradually to the more difficult. Indeed, I have often found that a novice was able to make, fill, and seal plain thermometer tubes the first day. The labour of operating the bellows for the smaller work is but slight, and scarcely calculated to tire even a young girl if continued all day; always assuming that the bellows are contrived to work efficiently and without considerable waste of energy.

An Aid in technical Education.—If technical education is, as almost all county councils have understood the term, not to be the mere teaching of trades as such, but rather the teaching of underlying principles, and such methods as may assist the worker in grafting upon his own trade the usages of other trades, glass-working at the lamp should take a leading place. Not only is it specially calculated to lead to an intelligent study of the reasons for and against various modes of manipulation, and to an appreciation of the importance of economy in effort, but there are very few industrial occupations which do not or cannot take direct aid from glass-working at the lamp. As a special preliminary training for specific trades or handicrafts, glass-blowing at the lamp may not only prove a useful aid to apprenticeship in the glass-house, but also serve as a means of giving the candidate for apprenticeship sufficient insight to really test his interest in the matter. To surgical and dental students, as also all students of the more delicate handicrafts, a preliminary training in glass-working should be specially useful, especially from the point of view of early acquiring ambidexterity.

The Origin of Glass.—Glass was probably made in the earliest times of which we have record, if we except the very first chapter in the mosaic accounts, for, as soon as men commenced to work the more refractory metals, coloured glasses must have been formed as slag. The epoch-marking discovery was doubtless the annealing of such glasses or enamels, but the discovery may have been brought about at a very early period by observation of the more stable character of such slags as cooled within the furnace, in comparison with similar slags cooled rapidly outside.

Ancient Egyptian Glass.—Glass beads found

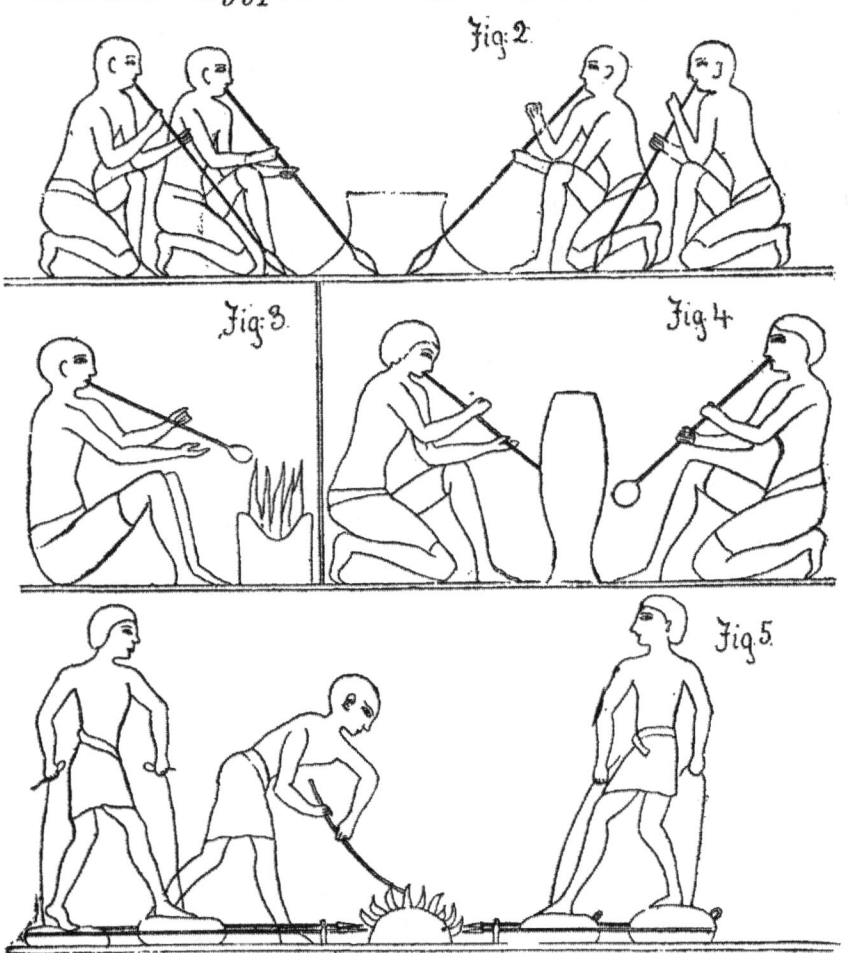

with mummies at Thebes take us back to the older Egyptian times, probably as far back as the time of the Israelites' captivity. The tomb-sketch (fig. 2) probably represents glass-workers of this period;

the representation being simplified by the omission of the blowing devices, and otherwise conventionalised after the manner of those who in our day represent industrial operations on monuments. Still the representation is unmistakable, as indeed are figs. 3 and 4; while the various older words which may indicate glass, and which occur in the Scriptures, are of doubtful significance, as they may mean natural crystals or such transparent stones as alabaster. We shall probably never know whether the Hebrew word (*zikukith*), which our translators of Job xxviii. 17 render crystal, and which Dr Martin Luther—possibly as a result of an unconscious effort to emphasise the sense—renders as diamond, really means glass; but the fact that the learned seventy of Alexandria about 300 to 200 B.C. rendered the word by the Greek *hyalos*, which at that time generally (and perhaps invariably) meant glass, counts for something; moreover, the reference to the tear bottle in Psalm lvi. 8 makes it tolerably clear that the use of the tear bottle was generally understood at the time the Psalms were written or collated (*circa* B.C. 1040). It is highly probable that at this period there were glass-houses in regular work in Egypt. The blowing for the more ancient Egyptian glass furnace, or rather hearth, was doubtless something of the kind shown in fig. 5, this, like the others, being from a tomb in Thebes. We see here four skins worked by two men, the pull up being by a cord or strap and the push down by the foot. One may suppose that as soon as the glass was melted and fit for working the bellows were removed. A blue scent-bottle, which undoubtedly belongs to the ancient Egyptian period of glass-making, is in the British Museum, and in this sense by "ancient" one means about the period of the captivity of the Israelites. To certain moulded beads, and I think also the blue scent-bottle, Garnier attributes the date 1650 B.C., which would be a little before the death of Joseph. All authentic Egyptian glass of this ancient period is, I believe, semi-opaque, enamel-like, or highly colored, and it includes copper red, a turquoise blue, green, cobalt blue, and silver yellow. We do not know when the revival of glass-making took place in Egypt, but it was undoubtedly after the conquest of Egypt by Alexander the Macedonian and the founding of Alexandria. Probably under the whole dynasty of the Ptolomies, a dynasty rather Greek than Egyptian, glass was made at Alexandria, a city which for nine centuries was the chief seat of learning and industrial progress. On the overturning of this dynasty in the time of Cleopatra (B.C. 30) and the reduction of Egypt to a Roman province, the glass industry doubtless received a new impulse, and from A.D. 117 to 273 the glass-houses of Alexandria were undoubtedly in very full work. Strabo, writing about the time of Christ, refers to glass-making in Egypt, and says that the Egyptians possessed a vitrifiable earth, without which they could not make their glass. Possibly this may have been an infusorial silica infiltrated with natural soda.

Pliny's Story and a Hebrew Version.—The story of Pliny the Elder as to the origin of glass is found in the school books, and is doubtless well worthy of the dubiousness with which Pliny gives it. Another story of a somewhat similar but less improbable character is told by Bernard Palissy in his *Traité des Eaux et Fontaines* (*circa*, 1577). He says the Israelites set fire to a forest, and one result was to so fuse together soda or nitre and sand that glass was formed. Palissy probably obtained this story from some Talmud or Hebrew writing, and it would be a matter of interest to find the original. Flavius Josephus mentions the incident.

Roman Glass.—The Emperor Nero obtained his finer glassware from the Alexandrian glass-works, but in his time glass-houses where coarse work was turned out existed in the neighbourhood of Rome. Very soon, however, the Roman artificers began to originate, and improved forms and colors were frequently put in the market and watched for with eager curiosity. The Barberini (Portland) Vase is a fine example of the skill of the old glass-workers, and as it was found in the tomb of Alexander Severus, who died A.D. 235, it may be looked upon as of the Alexandrian period, taking this term in its widest sense and looking on the Roman glass-houses as one in sequence with the Alexandrian. Little advance of fundamental importance has been made in ornamental glass-work since this period, excepting that production has been cheapened, and certain chemicals being in a purer state, brighter colours and clearer bodies can be produced.

The Venetian Period.—The drift of industry towards the north of Italy which took place as the Roman Empire disrupted took the glass manufacture with it, and glass-works were established on the refuge islands bordering on the Adriatic, where all the staples for glass-making were to hand. In the thirteenth century, Venice supplied Europe with all the finer glass, and maintained its supremacy until our Tudor period. The magnificent mirror plates and cut borderings now to be seen in Hampton Court Palace are a good illustration of what Venice supplied between three and four hundred years ago. Although the Venetian factories still exist and produce remarkable and interesting work,—work done by artists who form a race of perhaps unbroken succession from the Alexandrian period,—Venice has now no commercial supremacy in the glass industry; unless perhaps in the matter of colored beads and a few special styles of fine work. In Egypt there are still glass-houses, but the industry is at its very lowest point, short of extinction.

Glass-Workers not mere Proletarians.—When a new industry makes its appearance it is often understood that even one who prides himself upon being better than the mere vulgar herd may labour therein without loss of self-respect, and without being degraded in the eyes of his fellows. It is now so with electric lighting; many who would scorn to be mere gasfitters, priding themselves on being electricians; and in the early days of printing, type-setting and press work were considered to be fitting occupations even for the noble and lordly. This sentiment had much to do with the establishment of the glass industries in the north of Europe, for Louis IX. of France (St Louis) declared glass-working to be an occupation in no way derogatory to the dignity of the nobility (*circa* 1250). Very little progress was made in France until the beginning of the fourteenth century, when Louis X. gave the members of the aristocracy special privileges in connection with the glass manufacture. It was, however, in the seventeenth century that large glass-houses were established in France, England, and other north European States, and as late as the beginning of the present century the glass-workers " in some British glass-works were commonly called ' gentlemen glass-blowers ' " (Parnell).

Our own Time.—The history of glass in our present century is but a chapter in the commercial history of the day. Means have been devised to work economically on a huge scale by the so-called tank furnaces and the re-generative system of gas-heating. Manufacturers now strive for economic production with the most rigid exploitation of the operatives; and a neglect of every idea of scientific progress, as distinguished from the struggle for immediate commercial profit, is characteristic of the time. We have no school for teaching glass-workers those underlying laws on which progress depends, nor public institution for research; and researches on glass, it must be remembered, may involve much of that which is too often deprecated as "waste" by the manufacturer. The manufacturer is himself, for the most part, helpless in the matter, as close competition, high railway rates, heavy taxation, and burdensome rents or establishment charges, often make his position more precarious and more dangerously verging on the balance than that of the proletarian. It is, therefore, not to be wondered at that he is unwilling to risk his existence by going far from the beaten path.

CHAPTER II.

The Kind of Blowpipe Flame suited for Glass-working. Various Blowpipes and Bellows. Position and Light for convenient Working.

The Characteristics of Flame.—It is very essential for the student not only to understand the general nature of the blowpipe flame, but also to be able to instantly recognise the ideal flame for glass-working when obtained. The conditions for obtaining this ideal flame are so narrowly limited that without special study it is easy to miss it altogether in rapidly changing a condition from one extreme to another.

A candle flame is shown in section by fig. 6. The dark portion marked A in the sketch and surrounding the wick is a hollow containing combustible gas. Nearly surrounding this non-luminous hollow is the bright portion of the flame (B); this being the region where imperfect or partial combustion takes place. A cold body placed in this luminous portion will receive a coating of carbon in the form of soot. Surrounding this luminous region is an outer tegument (C), shown by a dotted line, and so faint in comparison with the luminous part that it may easily escape notice altogether. This outer portion or region of complete combustion is nevertheless the hottest part of the flame, and a very thin platinum wire carefully held at the right distance over the luminous part of a candle flame will melt to a globule. In order to render this very faintly luminous part of the candle flame distinctly visible to the eye, hold a lump of common salt at D so that it is just short of touching the luminous part of the flame. The sodium of the salt will now tinge the outer tegument of the flame yellow, and render it distinctly

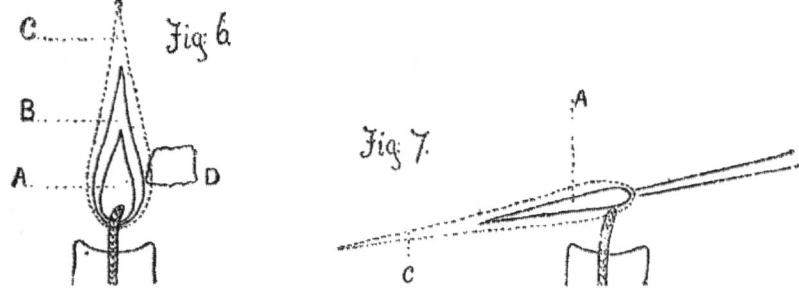

visible. If now we direct a blast of air through the candle flame by a fine jet, as shown by fig. 7, the luminosity of the flame is almost destroyed, and the tegument, previously almost invisible, becomes distinctly visible if the experiment is made in a place not too brightly illuminated. We now have but two regions in the flame, the hollow part, A (fig. 7), and the region of complete combustion, C (fig. 7); this latter being now much elongated and extending inwards as far as the hollow. It is this region of complete combustion which is the working part of the blowpipe flame, and a simple blast of air from a fine and interiorly smooth jet across a candle flame is quite good for glass-blowing, excepting that it is only large enough for the most miniature work, and is mechanically inconvenient, as the candle in burning down disturbs the adjustment of the jet.

Gas the most convenient Fuel.—A gas flame has the very great advantage of being more constant in its relation to the air-jet than is possible with any flame depending upon a wick; hence it is that, where gas can be obtained, all glass-blowers but the most conservative use it. At the same time it must be remembered that the blowpipe flame obtainable when an oil or tallow lamp is used should be fully equal to that from gas. In the hands of a skilled worker the oil or tallow lamp may even be a little superior to gas; but more skill is required in adjusting the lamp, and frequent re-adjustments are necessary.

Fundamentals of the Gas Blowpipe.—The gas flame, suitable for the production of a blowpipe flame, is one obtained by the flow of gas through a rather large aperture, and when no air-blast is driven through the gas the appearance is as shown at fig. 8. This figure also shows two air-jets, A and B, in position; either one of which might serve to convert the luminous gas flame into a satisfactory blowpipe flame. When the blast of air is directed across the mouth of the gas-pipe, this latter may, with advantage, be pinched in a little, as shown in fig. 9, where one is supposed to be looking down on the gas outflow; and the air-jet is shown in section. The best form of the blowpipe flame is also here indicated. To obtain this the air-jet must be adjusted by trial, both as regards distance and centring; a mere mechanical centring being unsatisfactory even when the air-jet is in the position B, fig. 8, as the blowpipe for glass-blowing is generally set not very much out of the horizontal

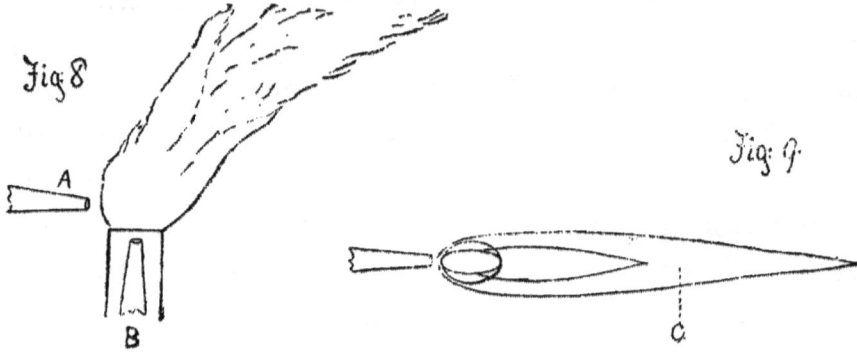

position, and the drift of the gas upwards has to be allowed for.

Criteria of the ideal Blowpipe Flame. — The appearance of the thoroughly satisfactory blowpipe flame or the ideal flame is very characteristic; the area of complete combustion, C, fig. 9, forms about three-fifths of its length, and has a peculiar reddish purple glow. The outline of the flame is smooth, and the flame rather recalls that of the oxyhydrogen blowpipe than that of the usual flame of the table blowpipe as met with in chemical laboratories and sketched in works on chemical manipulation. The chief criteria of excellence are: (1) that a thin platinum wire instantly fuses in any part of the region of complete combustion, C; and (2) that a bead of flint-glass does not suffer reduction or blackening in any part of the region C. If the flame is anywhere rough in its outline, or unsymmetrical in shape, glass containing lead (flint-glass) cannot be worked in it without blackening; unless, indeed, the glass be held so far outwards towards the point as to be very badly placed in relation to the heat. This flame, which I may call the ideal flame or the flame of complete combustion, is only perfect within such a narrow range of adjustment that any want of symmetry involves imperfect combustion at some part of the circumference, and where imperfect it will reduce glass containing lead. The flame may be made unsymmetrical by reason of a very little local roughness of the inside of the air-jet, and to avoid trouble from this source many of the most successful glass-blowers use a piece of glass-tubing for the air-jet, as will be described farther on. If the air-jet is too far back, the flame will be rough at the tip and will give a roaring note from partial extinctions, rapidly following each other; if the air-jet is a little too much forward, the flame becomes long and pointed, and often there will be some of the luminous flame remaining around the jet. When the air-jet is much too forward, the air blows quite through, and the flame becomes tubular. The pressure obtainable with the bellows ordinarily supplied for laboratory purposes is usually insufficient for the production of more than a small flame of the character referred to above, and, moreover, to maintain such a flame involves very constant pressure, as if the flame changes at every stroke of the bellows there is little hope of a satisfactory result, and the blackening of flint-glass is almost inevitable.

Flint-Glass a Test of the Flame.—When flint-glass is worked one of three things must happen: (1) the glass is heated fully and satisfactorily in an ideal flame; (2) the glass is blackened, and when this happens it is always heated less satisfactorily than in the first case; (3) the glass is not blackened, but is held so far in front of a bad flame as to be very unsatisfactorily heated. As the flame which is ideal for flint-glass is also the hottest, and best suited for glass not containing lead, I always give a beginner flint-glass to work, and let him use this until he has learned to properly adjust and maintain the flame.

A standard Blowpipe for general Use.—Having indicated the kind of flame which must be produced, the criteria by which that flame can be recognised, and the main principles to be observed in securing it, I will next describe various forms of blowpipe, commencing with a pattern which I have arrived at after many changes, and which I look upon as my standard blowpipe for use with gas.

Fig. 10 is a general perspective view, and in fig. 11

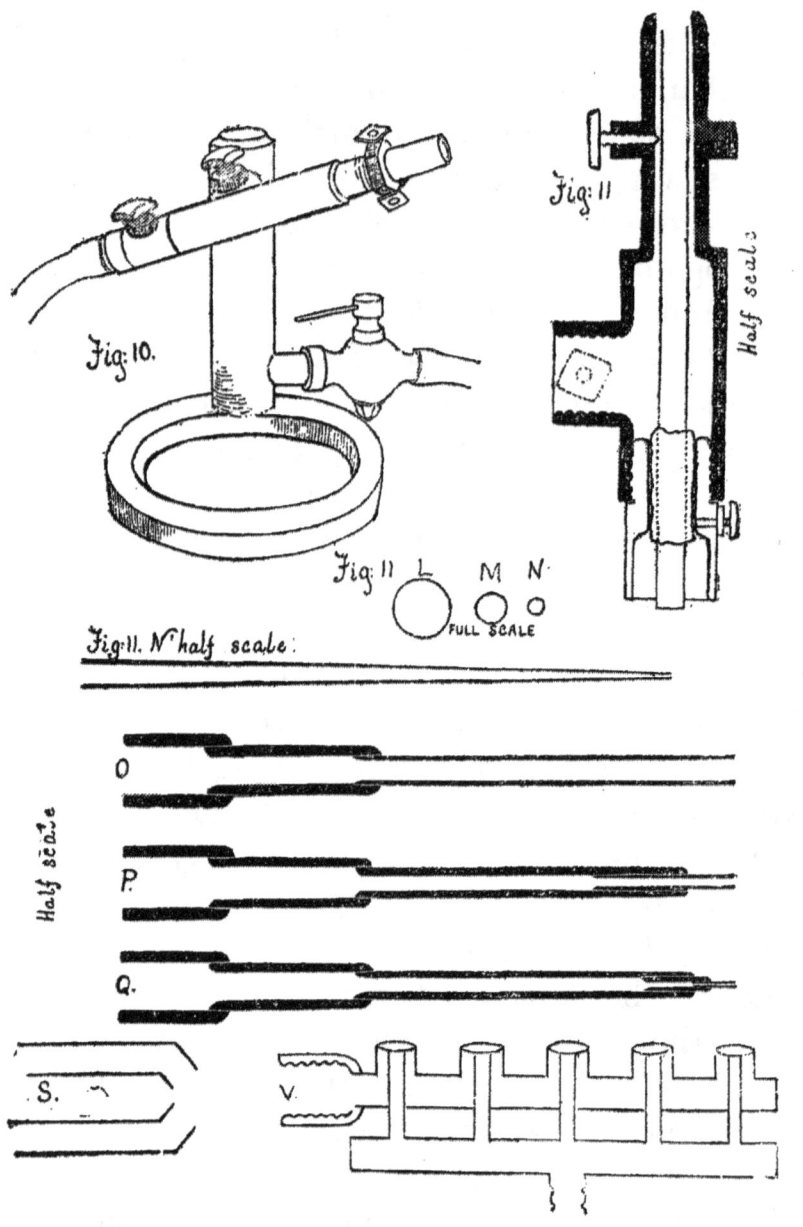

the blowpipe itself is shown in free or supplemented section on a scale of one-half the actual size. Fig. 11 is an iron gas-pipe tee for $\frac{1}{4}$-inch size, which is mounted, as shown in fig. 10, to swing in a vertical plane on the support; which support is a piece of $\frac{3}{8}$-iron gas-pipe brazed to an iron ring. This iron plate serves as a foot or as a means of fastening to a bench. The top of the upright is closed by a disc of iron brazed in, and close under this disc is brazed in a $\frac{1}{4}$-inch nipple, upon which the tee trunnions; a pinching screw, serving to fix the tee at any required angle. The inlet for gas at the bottom of the pillar is provided with a stopcock, having a long arm for easy adjustment. Into the tee, fig. 11, is brazed the nose; this being a short piece of $\frac{1}{4}$-inch gas-pipe shaped as shown, bored smoothly to a caliber of $\frac{5}{16}$ of an inch, and bearing a hexagon nut in the position shown (brazed on). Three screws for centring the air-jet pass through the alternate faces of this nut. This centring must be by trial with the flame, as the upward drift of the gas is a disturbing element which renders a mere mechanical centring unsatisfactory. The fitting which carries the air-jet is shown (fig. 11), and consists of an iron nipple brazed into a short length of smooth brass or gun-metal tubing. This or the nipple receives the air-jet, and when this air-jet is of glass it is fitted by means of a flexible setting, such as a short bush of india-rubber tubing. At the side of the tube, H, is brazed a block through which passes the pinch screw; which is used when brass jets are employed.

The best possible jet is a glass tube, as shown (fig. 11), cut off sharply at the fore end. Full instructions as to cutting off will be found farther on, so here it will be sufficient to show at L, M, N the actual sizes of the three jets which it is convenient to have. The largest glass jet, L, should be a piece of tube parallel throughout its length, and the intermediate jet, M, may be so or may taper slightly, but the smallest jet, N, should taper a little, as is the case if drawn out of a larger tube. N shows (half scale) a convenient section. As the glass jets are liable to be broken it is well to have an alternative set of brass jets, shown (half scale) by O, P, Q, which can be conveniently made of brass tubing as shown, soft soldering being in this case sufficient, as the tube carrying the air-blast never becomes hot, and brazing or hard soldering cannot be done without oxidising and making rough the inside of the tubes. Internally smooth tube should be used (Smith's Metal Warehouse, St John's Square, Clerkenwell), and every care should be taken to fit the tubes together centrally. Such air-jets are rather more trouble to make than drilled-out jets, but, as far as my experience goes, the jets built up of smooth tubing are essential if one wishes to have a blowpipe which is thoroughly efficient, and at the same time small in size. Smallness in size is a most important element from the point of view of the free use of the hands, wrists, and arms. Although taper jets shaped like N, fig. 11, and made of sheet-brass with a brazed seam, are fairly good if broached out smooth and true inside, they are troublesome to make, and do not give so smooth a flame as a parallel jet. The very worst kind of jet I have tried is one contracted at the orifice like S, a kind often found on commercial blowpipes, and sometimes a cap of similar shape constricts the gas outlet. Such jets produce rough flames in which heat is wasted, and in which flint-glass cannot be satisfactorily worked. If all the brass jets fitted to the above described blowpipe are so made that the external diameter is the same in each case at the place where the centring screws bear, much time will be saved in changing jets. Still it must be remembered that this blowpipe is one with which an instantaneous change from jet to jet cannot be made, but is an inexpensive single instrument for all-round work, which, if carefully adjusted, will give an ideally perfect flame. By unscrewing the blowpipe, other fittings may then be screwed on the standard. The most important of these are the fish-tail burner, a bunsen burner, or a multiple blowpipe, V, fig. 11. This latter is sometimes used in drawing out small tubes from large tubes, and in making bends of a certain class.

That flame in which perfect adjustment is of the most essential importance is the largest flame as obtained with the glass air-jet, or the brass jet, O, as at least 99 per cent. of the work is done with this large flame. I, therefore, give in fig. 12 a full-size sketch of the essential part of the blowpipe as fitted with this jet, everything being so carefully drawn to scale that if the plan is followed and the instructions as to air pressure and gas are attended to, a satisfactory result is fairly certain. The reference letters are the same as in fig. 11, and the air-jet shown in position is a piece of glass tube very thin

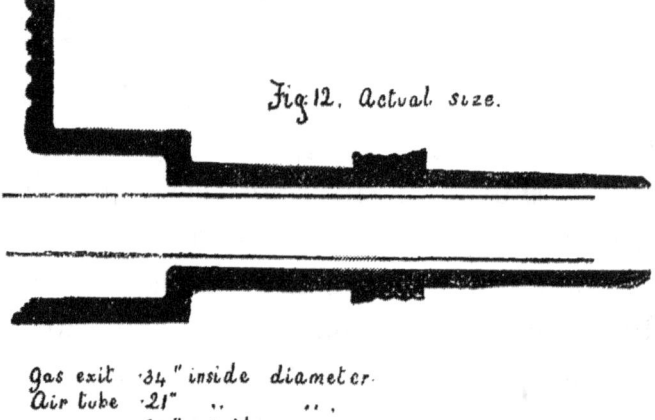

Fig. 12. Actual size.

Gas exit ·34" inside diameter.
Air tube ·21"   „   „
  „   „ ·24" outside   „
  „   „ terminates ·2" from gas exit.

in the side; in fact, it cannot be too thin, and the bushing of rubber tube which holds it in place in the nipple, fig. 11, should be so loose as to allow easy play under the centring screws. This tube must be very carefully selected for roundness, uniformity of thickness in the side, and freedom from lumps or knots. The ends, and more especially the forward end, must be cut off quite squarely across, and the sharp edge must not be removed by melting. Directions as to cutting off the glass tube will be found on p. 78, and it **may** be remarked that it is no easy matter to obtain a division of the tube sufficiently regular or even for a good jet; and when a suitable length of tubing is found it is well to cut it into pieces of the right length and preserve them as reserve jets. The glass jet is not liable to melt at the end by the heat, as the blast of air keeps it cool. Occasionally, a small chip flies off and the jet becomes useless; but careless use of the centring screws is the most usual source of fracture.

It will be noticed that the outer tube for the gas is very much smaller than in the case of most blowpipes for a full-sized flame; that is to say, the largest flame which can be conveniently maintained by means of the foot bellows; but the annular space indicated in fig. 12 will, if the gas supply is good and a large tube supplies up to the inlet, pass far more gas than is ordinarily required. If the air pressure is equal to $\frac{1}{4}$ lb. on the square inch, the gas will have to be turned down until the flame is about $4\frac{1}{2}$ inches long to get the ideal kind of flame, and this flame will consume about 13 feet of gas per hour. If now the pressure is increased to $\frac{1}{2}$ lb. on the square inch, a flame of the ideal character and about 6 to 7 inches long is obtained with a gas consumption of about 25 feet per hour. To maintain double this pressure with the glass jet in question, or a pressure of 1 lb. per square inch, is hard work with a foot bellows; but we thus obtain the largest flame which it is practicable to maintain by foot power, a flame 10 or 11 inches long and consuming 50 or 60 feet of gas per hour, a flame not only suited for blowing heavy bulbs having a capacity of a pint or more, but useful for brazing large work and for fusions. Ten lbs. of brass can be easily fused with this flame if proper jacketing is used for the crucible. When the blowpipe is to be used up to this power an increase in the size of the actual outflow annulus should be the last means resorted to for facilitating a flow of the gas. The supply-pipe should be large up to the blowpipe, and the inside of the nose of the blowpipe should be polished with fine emery applied with a longitudinal motion. The glass jet is quite essential for the highest power with this blowpipe, as not only does the glass tube pass 20 or 25 per cent. more air than any metal tube of similar size which I have used, but its outside smoothness serves to ease the passage of the gas. The small blowpipe just described performs better for gas furnace operations than any one of several dozen blast burners of large size and uncertain action which now lie discarded in my laboratory; the sole exception being the blast burner, with multiple jets of the late Mr John J. Griffin; which burner is described and figured on p. 785 of vol. ii., 1866 edition, of Watts's *Dictionary of Chemistry*. It was a study of the performance of this burner and of Griffin's still unrivalled blast gas furnace which led me to construct the blowpipe above described; the essential point of which is a strictly parallel outflow of air and gas, whereby the air supply may be increased, and the air-jet set far back, without blowing out the flame or producing a rough flame with irregularly distributed reducing areas, which disintegrate flint-glass, even if no ultimate blackening is noticeable. See page 196. At the same time I assume that the beginner will often find it convenient to purchase a blowpipe with a metal jet, and the above description will, at any rate, serve as a guide in selection.

The rapid Change from large to small Jet.—For certain classes of glass-work, perforation for instance, it is essential to have a small flame, and from what has been said above it is evident that mere turning down of the large flame will not completely meet the case. The several jets shown in fig. 11 provide for flames of various size, but they cannot be changed with that rapidity which is very desirable. When one is doing work which frequently necessitates a small flame it is often convenient to have a second blowpipe standing ready, but every additional fixture on the working-table is an obstruction, hence a blowpipe which will give a change of flame by one movement becomes very desirable. As far as I know, the first blowpipe of this character was devised by Mr Gimmingham, but the form described below is, I think, less obstructive to manipulation and more convenient. Altogether it forms a very compact, useful tool for general glass-blowing, and, as shown in fig. 13, it is the outcome of many modifications and trials. I think it gives three flames as near perfection as is practicable with metal jets, and the absence of such centring screws as are shown by fig. 11.

The Author's rapid change Blowpipe.—The body of the blowpipe (fig. 13) is a large stopcock, the plug of which has a disc, A, for turning at the small

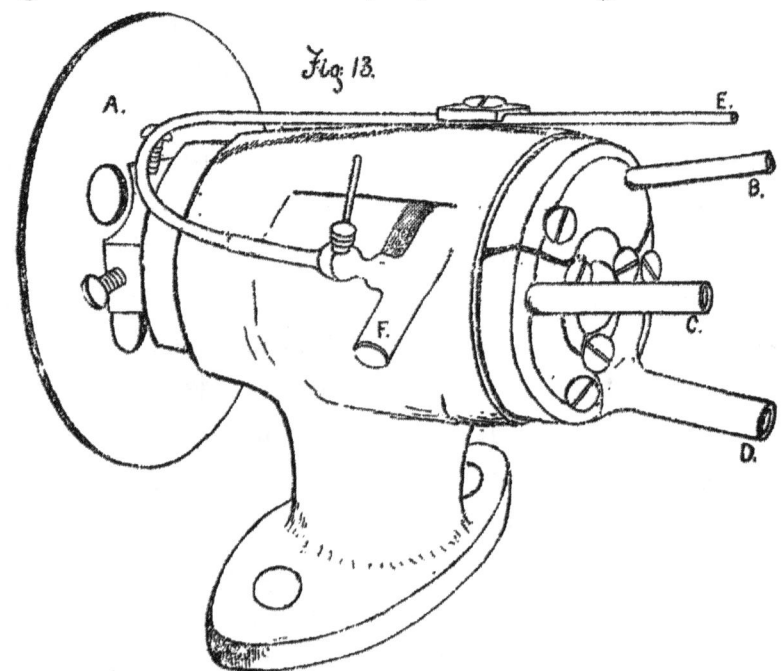

end, and three blowpipes, B, C, D, at the large end; either one of which, when brought to the top, becomes connected with air and gas-supply, and is lighted by the kindling jet, E. Air enters by a hole at the base of the main pillar, and gas enters by the short branch shown at F. The sketch forming fig. 14 will make the construction sufficiently clear to enable a mechanic to construct it. In fig. 14

the blowpipe is shown in modified section on a scale of half linear. A groove, G, turned in the plug, allows the air to reach the receptacle, H, and, as shown, the plug is in the position for supplying the central jet of D with air. The dotted circle, I, shows where the gas-supply enters the plug and passes to the outer tube of the blowpipe. As all three jets are similar in character but different in

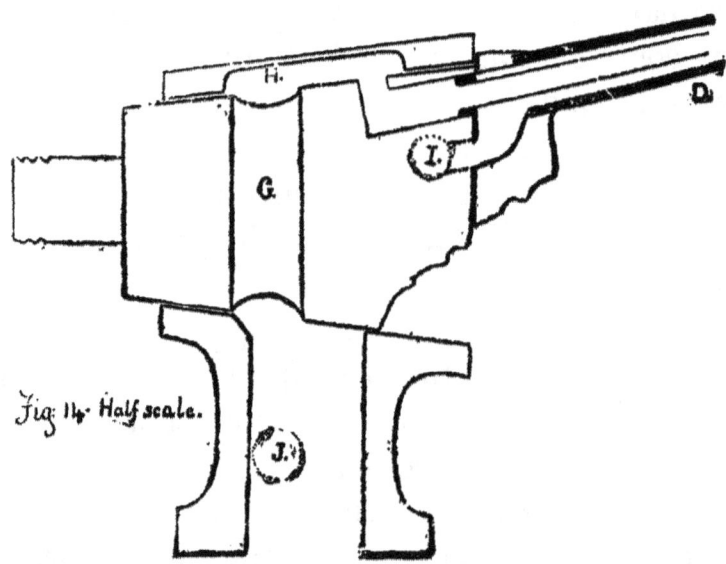

Fig. 14. Half scale.

size, the one position shown in fig. 14 sufficiently illustrates all. The special advantage of the disc, A, fig. 13, as against any form of cross or bar, is that it always presents the same figure to the left hand (or even the wrist) when it is adjusted, and the gas holes in the plug are so arranged that the gas-supply can be entirely cut off before the air-supply is affected. Consequently, the fine supply of the gas is readily controlled by the disc, A.

Sometimes it is desirable to control the **air-supply** by a stopcock, and to provide for this a large-bore stopcock is screwed in the standard. It is not shown in fig. 13, as it is on the side away from the observer, but its position is indicated by the dotted circle, J, fig. 14. When the air-supply comes by way of this stopcock, the hole at the base is closed by a cork or india-rubber plug; but my ordinary use of the blowpipe is with the air-supply coming from a vertical nipple in the top of the table, and in this case the stopcock, J, may be an outflow to another blowpipe (such a full-power blowpipe as fig. 12 for instance) or to some other device, as a fan motor for winding glass thread.

Various Blowpipes and Blowpipe Lamps.—It is not necessary to give full descriptions of other blowpipes and lamps, but the following short notes to figs. 15 to 25 may be useful:—

Fig. 15 represents a small inadjustable blowpipe, very easily made by brazing **an air-jet** into a brass elbow such as is used by gasfitters. It is convenient to have a few of these with **air-ways** of varying size. Such blowpipes are specially useful for work on fixed apparatus, the blowpipe being held in the hand; in such cases it is obviously best to avoid adjustable parts which may be dragged out of proper relation by the pull of the rubber tubes. 15A is a small portable blowpipe in which the flame is from a tuft of cotton saturated with spirit or petroleum, and is convenient for sealing off in Sprengel pump work; obviously—when practicable—an air-blast from the mouth is desirable when such portable blowpipes are used.

Fig. 16 shows an arrangement often used by the French glass-blowers, who frequently prefer to blow across the gas flame, rather than by an air-jet con-

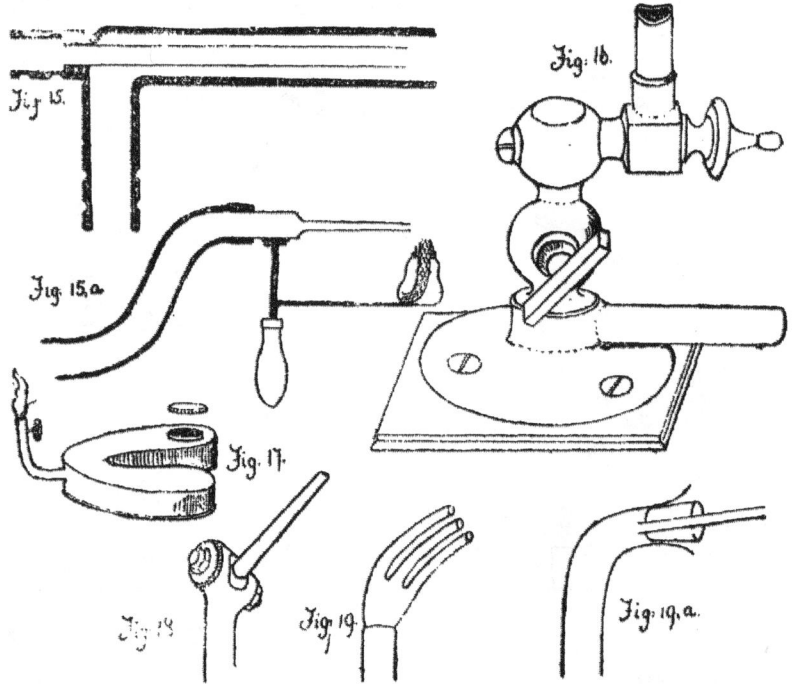

centric with the gas tube. This preference is probably rather the result of the ease with which the gas can be exchanged for the petroleum lamp, fig. 17, than from any opinion as to the advantage of the non-concentric arrangement.

Fig. 17 shows a form of lamp for paraffin oil; lamps similar to this being largely used in Paris,

It is sometimes made with three wick tubes, for use with such a triple air-jet as is shown by fig. 19. The horse-shoe shape of the body is an important feature in oil lamps, as it allows a free shifting of the lamp in relation to the air-jet.

Figs. 18 and 19A show air-jets intended to be mounted in the top of the bellows table, and to be used with figs. 16, 17, 21, or 23. Other forms are

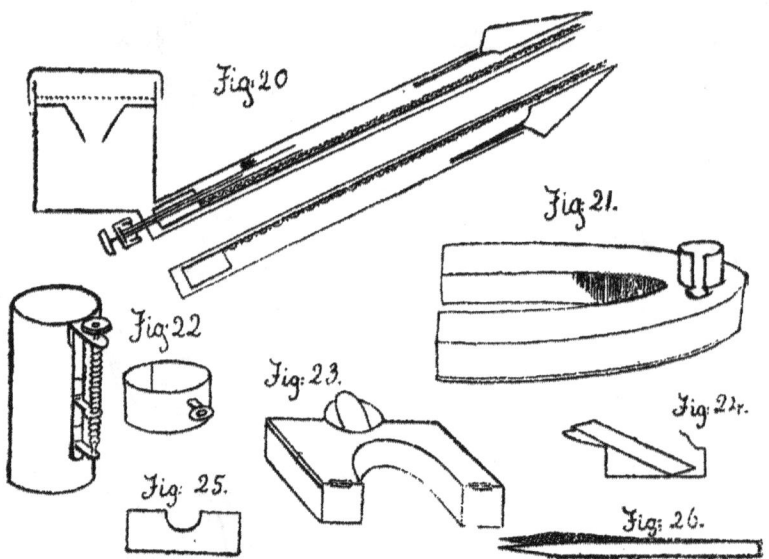

in use; a jet with a ball and socket joint being preferred by some. Fig. 19 is a multiple form sometimes used with the lamp having three wicks and mentioned above; at other times with a lamp like fig. 23, having a broad-plaited wick.

Fig. 20 represents a concentric blowpipe for use with paraffin oil, oil of turpentine, or even methylated spirit; although this latter fuel is not very suitable. The smaller air-jets are not shown, and the diagram needs no special explanation. A very perfect flame may be obtained with this blow-pipe.

Fig. 21 shows a convenient form of oil lamp, and 22 shows a screw adjustment for the wick. The construction in each case is made sufficiently obvious by the sketch.

Figs. 23, 24, and 25 show a simple form of blow-pipe lamp for oil; moreover, a form very suitable for tallow, a fuel preferred by many to the more fluid of the fatty oils. The projection of the wick over the front is a convenience, as allowing of the free moving about of the piece upon which work is being done. This lamp consists merely of a horse-shoe shaped vessel of tin-plate, having a spoon-like nose in front. In this spoon-like nose rests a tin-plate gutter which takes the wick (see note below on the wick), and this gutter may be small or large according to the wick used. As a rule, the wick will not tend to fall back into the body of the lamp, but the wire point used to trim it may be used to skewer the wick up to the required height. In fig. 24 the arrangement of the gutter and wick is shown separately. To control the size of the flame, a loose piece of tin-plate (fig. 25) is laid on the top of the lamp and pushed more or less forward. For trimming the lamp it is convenient to have, in addition to the pointed wire, A, a rather large pair of jeweller's steel corn tongs (fig. 26). When other fuel than gas is used, I think the balance of advantage rests with this last simple form of lamp and the use of tallow as a fuel.

When colza oil is used in a lamp having brass fittings, the getting of the affair into working order after being set aside for some months is a troublesome matter, as the oil becomes resinified, the brass corroded, and the wick takes an aggravating condition of glutinosity. Nothing of the kind happens with tallow, and if a full lamp (free from brass fittings) is put away for twelve months or more it is likely to be ready for immediate use when the tallow is melted. An incidental advantage of the tallow is that when cold it forms with its lamp a solid block, not liable to cause mischief when turned over, and free from that settling dust which sinks into oil. Still the odour from the tallow lamp is regarded as unfragrant by many.

When oil or tallow is used the wick is an important factor. In the case of the paraffin lamps, figs. 17 and 20, it does not much matter how hard and close in texture the wicks are; but in the case of the fat-oil lamps, fig. 21 and fig. 23, the wick must be of the loosest possible texture, and good wick cotton is not easy to get. For fig. 21, in which a liquid fat oil is supposed to be used, the wick cotton is made up into a round bundle, but in the lamp, fig. 23, in which the more solid oil (tallow) is used, the wick cotton must be plaited so that it will hold together in the open groove.

The Bellows.—The old-fashioned pear-shaped

bellows stands at the head of all kinds for efficiency, although special exigencies may make it desirable to use other kinds occasionally. The glass-blower, who uses his bellows almost all day long, cannot afford to use a bellows which is wasteful of energy, and I will begin by describing the bellows which I have found most satisfactory for ordinary work, and which I can operate all day without fatigue. The consumption of energy for an ordinary blowpipe flame (as specified on p. 31, and burning about 13 feet of gas per hour) is about 20 Watts, or, say, 15 foot pounds per second. Into the next section I propose to interpolate much as to the general principles of design and construction, so that this description of what I look upon as a carefully matured and efficient form for the glass-blower becomes, to some extent, a discursive chapter on bellows generally.

An efficient Bellows for ordinary Work.—The plan of my ordinary bellows is shown by fig. 27, and the shape is the old shape of the smith's bellows, appreciably longer than the domestic bellows, and much longer in form than the modern " Portable Forge " form, fig. 28. The latter is quite allowable when it is desired to put a bellows of high capacity under a table of very restricted size. Bellows still more shortened are now much in demand for occasional workshop use, this shortening being carried to an extreme in many commercial forms more or less resembling fig. 29. Such forms, although inconvenient for long-continued work, less efficient and less durable than the longer forms, offer considerable practical advantages for occasional opera-

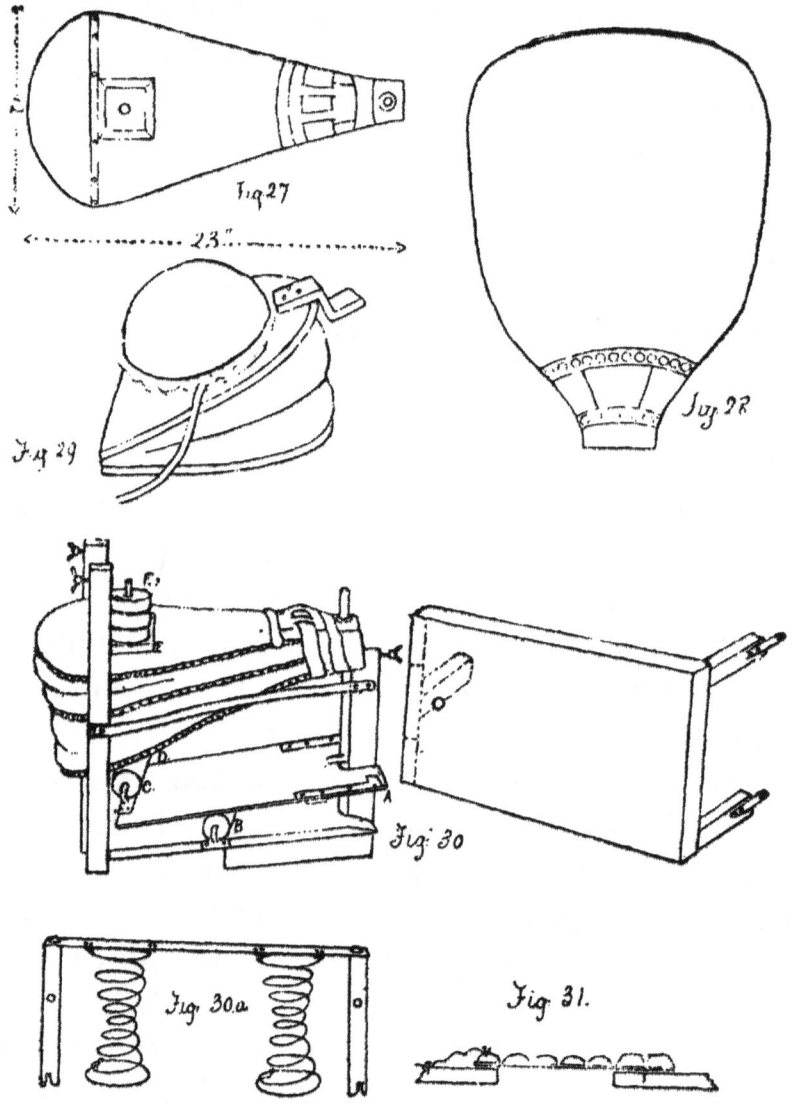

tions, when portability and the possibility of using in awkward positions are chief considerations. Such bellows have, therefore, but secondary interest from the glass-blower's point of view. As a rule, a bellows of this kind works independently of gravity, and can be operated sideways or inverted if needful, this involving the use of springs. The spring opening the feeder is frequently so strong as to waste much energy; but, considering the varied uses to which such a bellows may be put, this must not be looked upon as an error committed by the maker. Still, in all cases where space is not limited, I would urge the old, long form.

The general mounting of my ordinary bellows is shown sufficiently by fig. 30. The top of the bellows table is made detachable for convenience of transit in case of demonstrations away from headquarters, and the two parts interlock for packing in a way which will be sufficiently obvious from a study of the sketch. The treadle, A, works on ball-bearings, B, and the motion is communicated to the bellows feeder by a roller, C, working on ball-bearings. Each chamber of the bellows opens to a width of $5\frac{3}{4}$ inches clear between the boards at the butt end, and closes to $1\frac{3}{4}$ inches clear between the boards, this giving a maximum play of 4 inches; considerably less than that of some of the very portable bellows of half the length. Both valves, complete with seating, are easily removable; the lower or feeder valve being set upon the block D, which block is fastened to the lower board of the bellows by four screws. The upper valve is on a tablet fastened down to the middle board with four screws, and becomes accessible from the top, the block E being removable. The air-way covered by the lower or feeder valve is $1\frac{3}{4}$ inches by 3 inches, and the valve is made as light as possible. The leather—which is soft sheep-skin, flesh side down—is backed by rods of wood glued on so that any part may act as a hinge. The construction of this valve is sufficiently indicated by fig. 31. The valve on the middle board is very different, as it covers a hole only $\frac{3}{4}$ of an inch square, and it is heavily loaded; a considerable weighting of the middle valve being—as can easily be shown—absolutely a factor in efficiency, and in a glass-blowing bellows a necessity to prevent that drawback which would otherwise take place when the foot is raised after the treadle, A, has been held down for some little while. The normal pressure, at which this bellows is intended to deliver air, is $\frac{1}{4}$ lb. to the square inch, although, for some purposes, it may be loaded to deliver at $\frac{1}{2}$ lb. The loading of the middle valve may always be so considerable, that when the pressure in the feeder is equal to the working pressure the valve is without tendency one way or other, leaving the excess pressure to drive the air through the hole. As the area of the hole is $\frac{9}{16}$ of a square inch and the bellows is intended for a minimum pressure of $\frac{1}{4}$ lb. on the square inch, the valve with its load may have a minimum weight of $\frac{9}{64}$ lb. or $2\frac{1}{4}$ oz., and more weight may be added if required; for example, a $2\frac{1}{4}$-oz. weight should the wind be used at $\frac{1}{2}$ lb. on the square inch. The weight is best placed well over the hole, and the hinge of the valve at such distance that it is scarcely a factor in influencing the virtual weight on the valve. In leathering so small a bellows it is well to use a somewhat lighter and softer leather than is ordinarily employed for forge bellows, a stiff and heavy leather meaning additional expenditure of power, and, in most cases, a shorter duration for the leather. Soft, brown sheep-skin, weighing about one pound to six square feet, answers well. Before being nailed on it should be damped, and in nailing on it should be stretched so as to set inwards a little. The top of the table—shown in fig. 30 as separate—is covered with asbestos millboard; this being sponged over with dilute indian ink to soil the whiteness. Round the edge is a narrow bordering of iron, which forms an edging about $\frac{1}{8}$ of an inch high round the table. This is useful not only to prevent articles rolling off, but also as giving a firm bearing in cutting tubes with the file, and in other cases. Weights are placed on the top board, leaden discs, which can be threaded on the pin, F, being very convenient. About 35 lbs. will be required for the normal pressure of $\frac{1}{4}$ lb. to a square inch, if the weights are placed as shown. Of course, a given weight would give far more effect if placed farther from the hinge, but it is not desirable to strain the hinge by an upward pressure. Although weights form the usual loading for the wind chamber of a bellows; when I use the above-described bellows and table away from home, I generally prefer to use springs; two strong sofa springs, engaged under a light iron bridge as shown at fig. 30, can be easily arranged to give about the normal pressure of $\frac{1}{4}$ lb. to the square inch. Although with the spring there must be a general rise in pressure as the expanding chamber fills, there is less irregularity owing to the entry of individual blasts of air from the feeder, as the inertia of the weight takes an appreciable time to overcome.

The lever-treadle action, with ball-bearings as shown, is very good and involves very little loss of energy; but when room allows a stirrup and rounce action, as indicated by fig. 32, is probably the best mechanical system for transmitting energy either from the hand or the foot to a bellows. Leather belts are generally best, and as the two discs of the rounce need not have the same radius, any desired change in rate is easy. If the stirrup is inconvenient a treadle, as shown by the dotted line A, can be used; the extra friction being very small if the centre is at a considerable distance. I would urge the desirability of considering all matters which may economise energy when work is to be frequent or for long periods.

Commercial blowpipe Tables and glass-blowing Bellows.—The long, pear-shaped form (fig. 27) is seldom adopted in the case of the light and portable glass-blowing tables sold by dealers in chemical apparatus, and among those supplied for laboratory or experimental purposes there is so wide a difference of efficiency as to necessitate some care in purchasing. As far as my observation goes, the tables with circular bellows, manufactured by M. Enfer of Paris, are by far the best, and these are sold by most London dealers in chemical apparatus, but usually they bear the name of the dealer and not that of the manufacturer. The disadvantages incident to a much shortened form of hinged bellows do not apply to the circular bellows, and where compactness and portability are chief considerations, the circular form appears to be the most desirable. A bellows of the circular form and having a small horizontal area may be the equivalent of a long bellows occupying seven or eight times the floor space, as there is scarcely any limit to the extent to which the circular form may be made to open. An inspection of fig. 33, which represents the usual form of M. Enfer's glass-blowing table, will enable this advantage to be at once recognised, and the convenience of being able to put the feet a little to the sides of the pillar containing the bellows is a consideration. Another advantage is the comparative lightness of the weight required. Still, where the bellows is to be a permanent fixture and space is not a consideration, I would recommend for efficiency the long, pear shape actuated by the rounce action shown in fig. 32.

48   COMMERCIAL BELLOWS.

M. Enfer makes a number of patterns of his blowpipe table with circular bellows, and figs. 33, 34, and

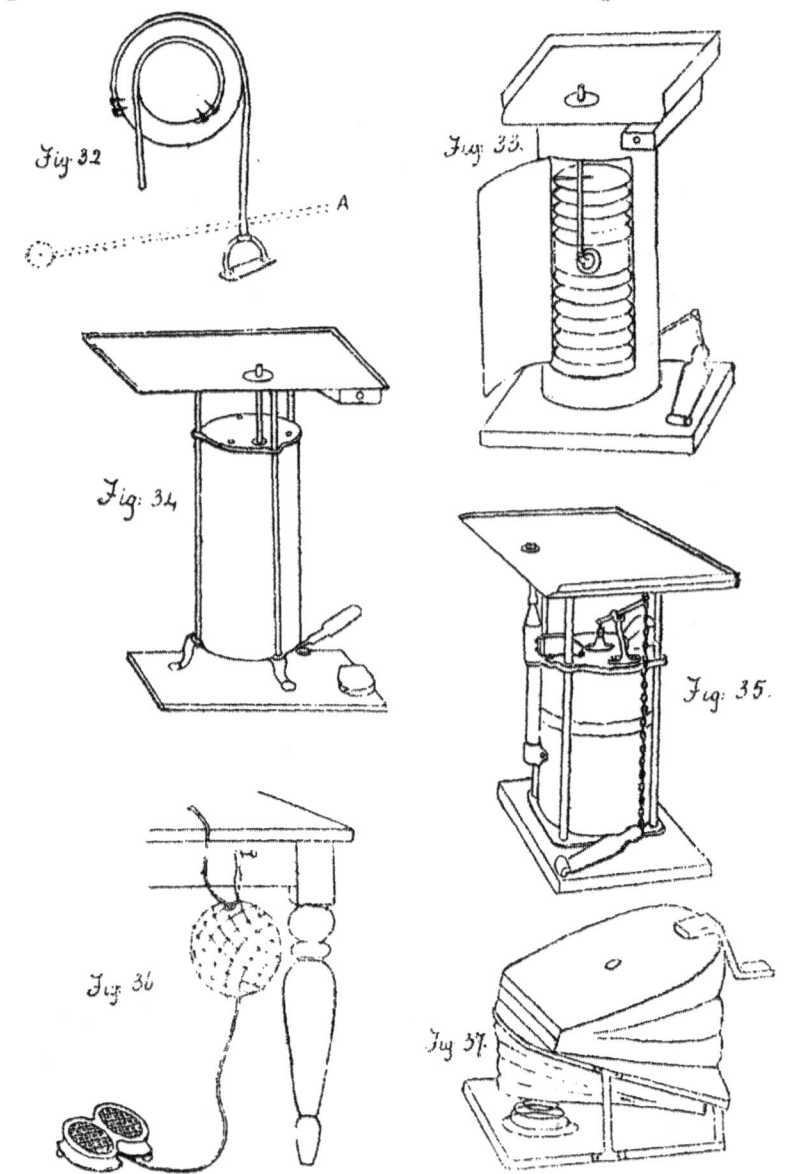

35 represent typical forms. Fig. 35 is a recent pattern, the full size of which, with bellows 10

inches in diameter, is adapted for the largest work which can be done with a blowpipe operated by the blast of a foot-bellows.

Various portable Bellows.—It is very often desirable to have a bellows which is not attached to the work-table and yet is provided with a treadle, so that it can be readily operated by the foot, and various portable forms of this kind are now obtainable at tool shops and at the dental depôts. As will be gathered from remarks already made, such bellows are often very ill-suited for the long-continued use involved in glass-working by reason of their mechanical inefficiency. A very small double-feeder bellows, obtainable at the dental depôts and tool shops, is remarkably efficient, but it involves a rocking action of the foot, as in working the domestic sewing-machine, a motion to which dentists are generally accustomed, but inconvenient at first to those who have been used to the ordinary workshop tools. This bellows, shown by fig. 36, is not adapted for producing a large blowpipe flame. Fig. 37 is a form sold at most cycle-material stores, and is generally subject to the fault of the spring which opens the feeder being much too strong. As the spring is generally inside, one has to cut a piece out of the top board of the bellows to get access to it, but this operation is an advantage if the opening is closed by a screw-on piece, as ready access to the valves is always desirable. Occasionally I have mounted a pair of small smith's bellows as shown in fig. 38, the feeder being uppermost and the air-chamber expanding downwards against a spring as in the portable bellows, fig. 37. The internal spring which lifts the feeder should not be too strong, and both valves should close with spring tension,—as slight as possible in the case of the upper valve and with considerable tension on the lower valve, this tension being determined as indicated on p. 44.

A Device for using ordinary domestic Bellows.— Two pairs of good domestic bellows mounted together,

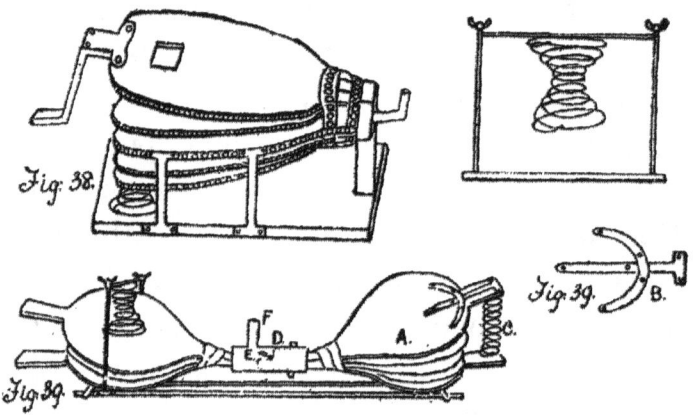

as shown by fig. 39, make by no means a bad combination for a medium-sized flame. The broad end of the feeder bellows, A, fig. 39, has two light frames made of steel bars brazed together, B, screwed on its upper and lower boards respectively; these frames extending over the handles of the bellows, and between these extensions is the coiled spring which keeps the feeder open. The lower frame gives a distance under the feeder which allows air to enter the valve. A second similar bellows is connected with the feeder by a brass tube, D, containing the valve, E, and provided with an exit tube, F. This second is the air-reservoir, and may be loaded by a weight or compressed by a spring; a convenient form of spring compress being indicated by fig. 39.

Oil for dressing Leather.—When the leather of the bellows becomes harsh and tends to fray where it folds, a little castor-oil should be rubbed on; the slightly-brown, hot-drawn castor-oil obtainable at the oil shops being as good for this purpose as the cold-drawn oil obtained from the druggist.

The Mouth as a Substitute for Bellows.—Glass-blowing without a bellows to urge the flame is scarcely practicable except for very small work, but a beginner may learn and study all the essentials under these circumstances. Only a small air-jet, say from a $\frac{1}{50}$ to a $\frac{1}{30}$ of an inch in diameter, can be supplied with air from the lungs. In learning to blow continuously with the mouth, the first matter is to acquire facility in breathing through the nose while the cheeks are distended. As soon as this habit is attained, a tube connected with a very small blowpipe jet is inserted in the mouth, and it will soon be found that a certain loss of air through the pipe can be supplied from the lungs without much effort, and without interfering with the breathing through the nose. As the blowing becomes less irksome a larger jet may be used.

Blowing by Power.—Except in large factories, organised for the production of special articles, as, for example, incandescent lamps, it is almost invariably the custom for each worker to supply his blowpipe with air by a foot-bellows. When power is used a piston-blowing machine is best, and as an air-vessel a chamber of concrete, strengthened with iron bars worked in the substance, is convenient. If about one cubic yard capacity is allowed for each blowpipe no expanding chamber is necessary, but it is convenient to have some device by which the pressure of the air automatically governs the engine. A pressure in the chamber of 2 or 3 lbs. on the square inch is desirable, and each worker must be provided with an easily-operated valve or stopcock.

Light and Position for Working.—The glass-blower should be seated either at a small table, at the end of a narrow table, or at a projection from a large table, so as to afford facilities for inclining long tubes to the flame. Most workers prefer the flame to point directly away from the seat, but, personally, I prefer it directed a little towards the right side. When the general illumination is very strong, it is difficult to judge of the flame and to see that front solid part which is the hottest. I prefer to work with my back or side to the window; the window being provided with a brownish yellow blind which can be drawn down. Close under the window it is convenient to have a table for incidental operations.

CHAPTER III.

Minor Tools and Appliances.

The File.—A very usual way of dividing the smaller glass tubing is to make a scratch or cut upon it with the edge of a file, and strain it at the marked place. The effective edge of the file wears down very quickly, but it may be restored by grinding one of the faces of the file, care being taken to use abundance of water on the grindstone to avoid softening the steel. The special conditions under which the file is superior to the tool next to be described are treated of on p. 80.

The Glass-Blower's Knife; two kinds.—An abrading or cutting tool with a very much keener and smoother edge than the file is useful for the larger sizes of glass tubing, especially thin-walled tubing such as is used in making test tubes, and such a tool is obtained by grinding a blade of steel to a suitable edge. A kind sold at chemical-apparatus shops is shown by fig. 40 and in cross-section at one end. It is made of steel of about the usual file hardness, and the edge is renewed on a rough stone like a scythe-stone, the knife requiring a frequent draw across the stone. This may be termed the soft knife in comparison with the instrument next described, which may be called the hard knife.

The hard Knife.—The hard knife must be made of a highly-carbonised steel, and must be hardened by being heated to bright redness in an iron box containing sufficient charcoal powder to cover it, and then being dipped in mercury which has been cooled to a temperature of about $-18°$ C. with a mixture of crushed ice and salt. The hard knife is conveniently made of a plate of steel $\frac{1}{8}$ of an inch thick and about the size of a gentleman's visiting card ($1\frac{1}{2} \times 3$ inches). One long edge is ground to an angle of $60°$ and the corners of the tablet are rounded off a little. After the hardening, the edge ground to $60°$ is finished off as smoothly as possible on an Arkansas oilstone. This knife—shown half-scale by fig. 41—can be safely carried in the waistcoat pocket, and is so carried by many glass-blowers, as the edge will not cut the hand, unless by very great carelessness. Obviously, the soft knife, with the rough edge given by a scythe-stone, can also be made in the visiting-card form, but the rough and somewhat more acute edge may cut the hand dangerously. The hard knife in its best condition is so brittle that it may break if dropped on a stone floor. The hard knife cannot well be made for a handle, as shown by fig. 40, as it would be likely to break off at the tang, unless partially softened, and softening is undesirable.

Iron half Circles for dividing Tubing.—These are made of iron wire about $\frac{1}{8}$ of an inch in diameter, and are represented by fig. 42. From

VARIOUS SMALL TOOLS.

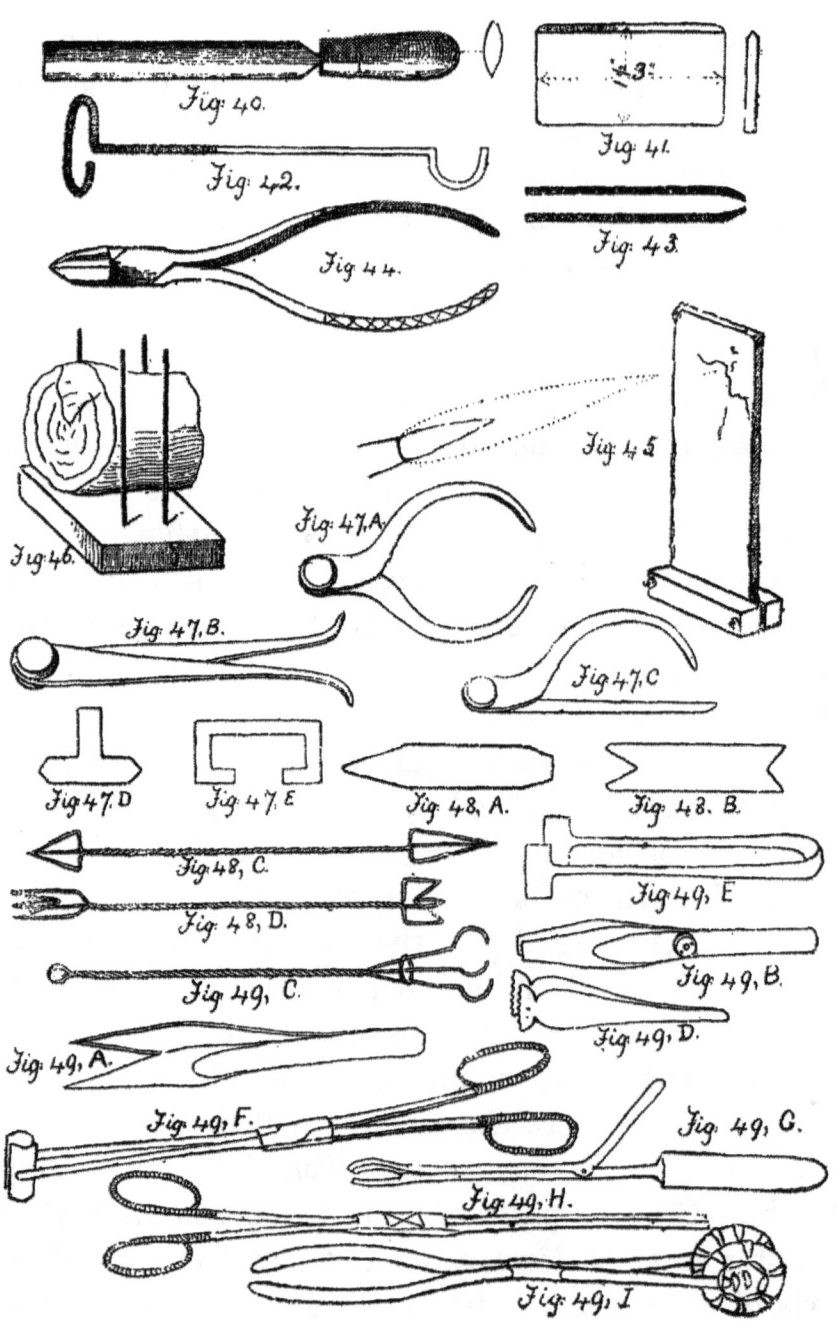

$\frac{1}{2}$ inch to $1\frac{3}{4}$ inches in diameter, rising by sixteenths of an inch, provides for all ordinary necessities. The cross and part of the shaft should be served with asbestos thread so that the tool can be held comfortably when the half circle is red hot.

Minute Gas-Jet for leading Cracks.—A piece of glass tubing about $\frac{3}{8}$ inch in diameter, drawn out and cut off as shown by fig. 43, is connected with the gas supply so that the gas burns at the drawn-off part. The point is now held in a bunsen-burner flame so as to soften it, when the jet will draw together and the flame of the outflowing gas will become smaller and smaller. When this flame is reduced to a length of about $\frac{1}{2}$ an inch, the glass is removed from the bunsen burner and the jet is allowed to cool, during which operation the hole generally becomes smaller—sometimes, indeed, closes altogether. If when finished the tube gives a flame $\frac{1}{4}$ of an inch long with the full pressure of gas, it will be about right. A jet regulated to size by turning down the gas at a stopcock is not satisfactory. When connecting the glass-jet, fig. 43, to a rubber tube, the gas should be turned on before the jet is connected, otherwise it may be some minutes before the air is expelled.

Berzelius's glowing-carbon Pencils for leading Cracks.—Sixteen parts of gum tragacanth are soaked in water so as to form a mucilage, and to this eight parts of gum benzoin dissolved in alcohol are added. These being well mixed in a mortar, finely-powdered charcoal (the fine powder obtainable from the druggist answers well) is mixed in until the whole is of a suitable consistency for rolling into sticks, which should be about $\frac{3}{16}$ of an inch in diameter. The above is Mohr's modification of the original instructions of Berzelius, but I have found it an advantage to make up the mucilage of tragacanth with equal parts of cold, saturated solution of nitrate of urea and water instead of plain water. The nitrate makes the pencils burn much more readily, and the reasons for preferring such a nitrate as nitrate of urea to nitrates of the fixed alkalies or nitrate of ammonia should be sufficiently obvious.

Scissors and Nippers.—The kind most useful for the trimming of hot glass is a pair of fine-pointed, embroidery scissors, although sometimes a pair of clockmaker's side-cutting nippers, fig. 44, are used.

Radiators.—When it is desired to use the heating power of a blowpipe to the utmost, a radiator of heat is placed just beyond the point of the flame. Perhaps the most convenient form is a strip of asbestos, about 2 inches wide and of convenient length, mounted between two clumps of metal which form a foot, as shown by fig. 45. When the greatest heat is required, as in softening a mass of glass for an exceptionally large bulb, a cross-section of charcoal, about 3 inches in diameter and mounted as shown by fig. 46, may be used. These radiators may be easily brought into position or pushed away as occasion requires. Short lengths cannot be

Callipers.—Fig. 47 shows the three forms of adjustable callipers required: A, outside; B, inside; C, thickness. The simple-hinged form without adjusting screw is best for ordinary work. Set callipers like D or E can be cut from sheet-metal as required for special work. The form E is generally required in couples, "pass" and "not pass" (see p. 106).

Turn-pins.—Solid turn-pins, fig. 48, or expanding cones are conveniently made from the carbon pencils used for the arc electric light, and are used in expanding the softened end of a tube. The female form, B and D, fig. 48, is not often used, but is specially convenient for certain purposes (see p. 130). The special advantages and uses of the two forms, skeleton and solid, are explained on p. 94 and p. 95. Skeleton turn-pins are made of iron wire brazed together where the ends meet and are then trimmed with a file (see fig. 48, C and D).

Various Tongs and Holding-Devices.—These are generally adaptations of commercial forms, and are brought into use as required. Fig. 49 shows a grouping of various forms which may be useful. The professional glass-blower often has no tongs except a pair of spring tongs like E, fig. 49. Tongs for holding hot glass should, when practicable, be served or covered with asbestos thread.

Shanks and Crushing-Pliers.—Irregular ends of

stout glass tubing may often be trimmed while cold by crushing the projecting parts with the optical shanks, fig. 50, A, but as one face of the glass to be crushed is concave an ordinary pair of pliers like fig. 50, B, is better.

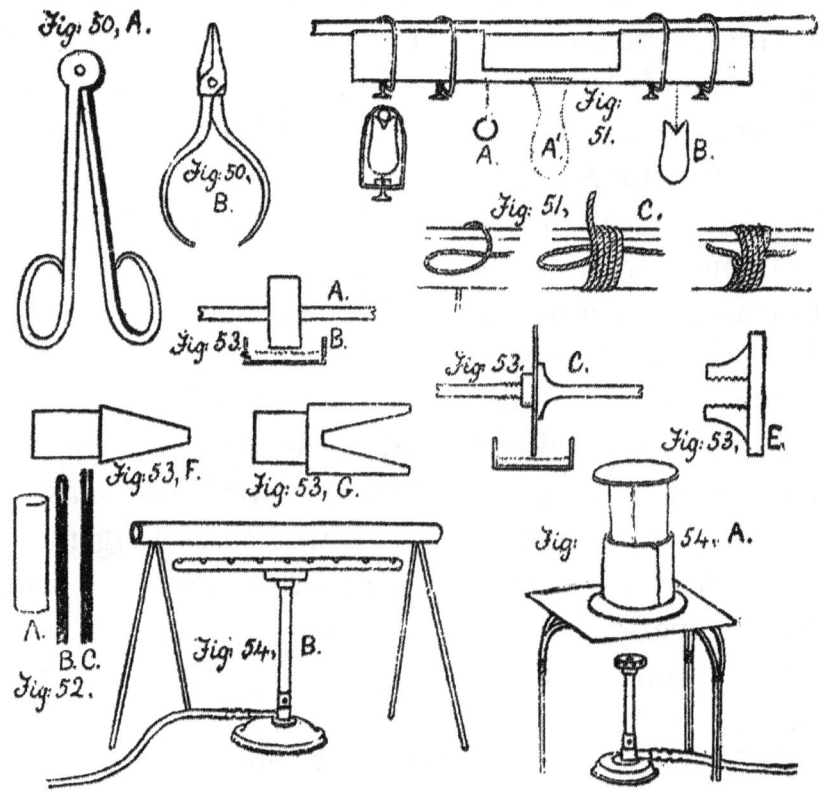

Branching Clamp.—When a thin tube is softened in the middle for joining on a branch, it is desirable to support the tube rigidly at the two ends. Fig. 51 sufficiently indicates the kind of clamp which is suitable. The main bar may be made of soft sheet-iron bent as shown in the sections at A and B.

The tube can be held down in the V groove by the screw eyelets shown, but it is often more convenient to tie the tube in position by string, the ordinary binding knot, the stages of which are shown at fig. 51, C, being used.

Tools for cleaning Glass-tubing.—The rammer by which a pellet of rag or paper is jumped through a long tube is simply a cylinder of copper, fig. 52, A; one $\frac{1}{4}$ of an inch in diameter by 5 inches long, and one $\frac{1}{2}$ an inch in diameter by 6 inches long, will serve all purposes. The cleaning bodkin is a copper wire having a long eye at one end, the eye being shown at fig. 52, B. The eye is made by sawing down through the wire as shown at C, and brazing the two ends of the cut portion together. A strip of rag being threaded through the eye, the outstanding ends are knotted or tufted as may be required. I devised this bodkin after trying many means for the quick cleaning of tubes, and after having experienced the inconvenience of the usual way of pulling a tuft of rag through the tube with a string.

Tools for grinding Glass.—A surface of type-metal, zinc, or copper, freely fed with a mixture of No. 80 (through sieve of 80 meshes to the linear inch) emery and ordinary paraffin oil, is perhaps the best means of smooth grinding glass, and for most purposes soft type-metal, such as is used in stereotyping by the paper process (four parts lead and one part antimony), is most convenient. A plain, flat grinding-slab is useful, but more commonly-used grinding-tools are shown in fig. 53, where A represents a cylindrical lap for the lathe, which should work in a trough, B containing the emery and paraffin, C a copper disc similarly mounted, E a facing disc to screw on the lathe, used in smoothing the ends of large tubes, also F and G male and female stoppering or stopcocking cones; these being most conveniently made of copper.

Annealing Ovens.—For objects tending rather to width than to length, such a form as fig. 54, A, is very suitable. A plate of stout asbestos millboard is laid on an iron plate supported over a bunsen burner, and upon this is set upright a rough tube of asbestos millboard, made by bending a strip and loosely binding round with wire. An extension piece of the same kind can be added as shown, and the top is covered by a second plate of asbestos millboard. This form is convenient as being readily and quickly adjustable, both as to diameter and length. The strips forming the body cylinders should obviously be so long as to form cylinders of the largest diameter likely to be required, and so thin as to coil to a much smaller diameter if need be, or several cylinders may be made in the first instance. The best Italian millboard about $\frac{1}{16}$ of an inch thick is suitable for the cylinders, but a stouter material is desirable for the top and bottom plates. Fig. 54, B, shows a convenient form for long articles,—an iron tube plugged loosely at each end with clay stoppers and supported over a gas-burner. Several of these ranging from $\frac{1}{2}$ an inch internal diameter to 2 inches may be provided, and sometimes they may be conveniently grouped on one stand; the burner being shifted laterally as required. Sometimes only one part of an article requires annealing, as, for example, that portion of an incandescent lamp into which the wires are sealed. In this case that portion which requires annealing may be made to project through a perforated cover into the body of fig. 54, A. For the systematic manufacture of similar articles annealing ovens are generally made so that when a new article is put in near the source of heat all others are shifted one degree away. A revolving device of this kind is easy to contrive, and one will be found described in Mr Rain's book on the incandescent lamp (see Bibliography).

Annealing is often done without any special oven being used, and this subject is generally treated of in another place (see p. 169).

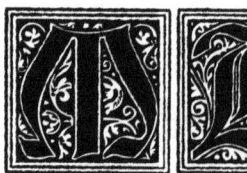

CHAPTER IV.

GLASS IN RELATION TO BLOWPIPE WORK. RODS AND TUBING. SYSTEM OF GAUGING. STORING, PRESERVATION, AND CLEANING.

Fused Silica as a Glass.—The ideal glass, as regards inalterability and hardness, is simply fused silica,—clear sand or quartz crystal fused at an intense heat. To fuse silica for the making of a pure silica glass, a large oxyhydrogen blowpipe is required, and the flame is directed downwards on a porous silica brick, previously heated to full whiteness. A small tank of the molten silica is thus obtained, and this tank must be fed with small pieces of silica,—best previously heated to whiteness. In this way I have found it by no means difficult to obtain a few ounces of thoroughly-melted, pure silica glass, but the working offers special difficulties which I need not enter into at present. For certain physical purposes, pure silica is probably the glass of the future. Mr H. L. Callendar, writing in 1892 (paper read before the Iron and Steel Institute, reprinted in *Engineering*, 17th June 1892, p. 762), makes brief reference to his attempts to work pure silica glass, and says:—" It has, in addition to its infusibility, physical properties of toughness and hardness and elasticity, which make it in every way superior to glass or porcelain for scientific purposes. Unfortunately, owing to the high temperature at which it softens, it is very difficult to work, and requires considerable skill. I have only as yet succeeded in making very small tubes of this material. With further practice and larger apparatus I hope, however, to be able ultimately to make tubes and bulbs of dimensions suitable for air-thermometer work." Leaving pure silica glass as at present standing outside ordinary practice, I propose to briefly consider the various glasses, the basis of which is silica in every case, but with such additions as render it more easily fusible.

Hard Bohemian Glass, known in the Laboratory as Combustion Glass.—This is the least fusible of the commercial glasses, and the silica is united with or softened by potash and lime;—the following being a representative recipe for glass of this character:—

>White Sand, . . 100 parts
>Carbonate of Potassium, 35 ,, to 40
>   (according to the fusibility desired)
>Chalk or Limestone, . 15 parts

The harder Bottle-Glasses and glasses used for water-gauge tubes on steam-boilers have rather variable composition, of which the following recipe is an example:—

Sand,	100 parts
Chalk,	35 "
Carbonate of Soda (Anhydrous),	20 "

Clay, marl, carbonate of strontium, wood-ashes, basalt, carbonate or sulphate of barium, and other materials locally available, enter into the composition of other bottle-glasses; the proportion of alkali can be reduced or increased according to the fusibility desired.

Crown, Sheet, and Plate Glass.—Although the term 'crown' originally indicated a method of making, it is now used to indicate a certain quality of glass which is easily fusible and ordinarily contains both potash and soda with a little lime. The following is a representative recipe :—

Sand,	100 parts
Carbonate of Potassium,	30 "
Carbonate of Sodium,	18 "
Chalk or Limestone,	13 "

The sheet glasses now largely made in Belgium and sent over here have a composition intended to give working qualities similar to the above, but the potash is reduced or omitted, and strontia or baryta are frequently employed, also, occasionally, white clay. Now that borax is cheap, a little is often added as it makes the glass flow readily. Plate glass is generally made a little more fusible to facilitate casting.

Soft German Glass for Tubing.—The soft German or Thuringian glass, of which much of the tubing for working at the blowpipe is made, has a composition generally similar to crown glass, but different samples vary considerably. Wood-ashes are frequently used in its composition as supplying a little potash, and a small quantity of black oxide of manganese is added to oxidise any trace of iron to the ferric state.

It is not by any means essential to introduce the sodium into glass in the form of carbonate of soda, the sulphate and even the chloride being often employed; but in these latter cases more considerable heating is required to drive off the electro-negative elements.

Flint-Glass or Lead-Glass.—The term flint-glass arose from the practice of using calcined, quenched, and crushed flints as the silicious base of the finer and more colorless glasses, and seventy years ago the only colorless glass easy to make was compounded of the purest silica obtainable (*c.g.*, the prepared flints, the purest sand or crushed quartz), oxide of lead and potash salts, as the carbonate and nitre. Such a flint-glass may be compounded as follows :—

Silica as above,	100 parts
Red Lead,	80 ,,
Carbonate of Potassium,	35 ,,
Nitre,	3 ,,

As a factor in the preparation of a colorless glass, manganese dioxide was much more important in the old days than now. The object of using red lead and nitre was to ensure oxidation of carbonaceous particles, but, as these materials are reduced rather easily, it often happened that in the end, such traces of iron as might be present existed in the ferrous state and tinged the glass greenish or brownish. A minute quantity of manganese dioxide was now added to oxidise the ferrous oxide to the ferric state in which its coloring power is much less. Manganese dioxide is especially suitable for this use by reason of the high temperature at which it gives up a portion of its oxygen. The manganese itself, if added in too large a quantity, would tint the glass amethyst color. In the old days soda was not used in making flint-glass, but the purer soda of the present day can replace potash without giving that green tint which was once believed to be characteristic of soda glasses, and much of the flint-glass of the present day contains soda, instead of potash as in the old times.

There are now many special glasses prepared for optical and other purposes, the consideration of which would be appropriate in a work on glass generally, but would occupy too much space in a work of the present character. Still among the Jena glasses there is one which possesses special advantages for the construction of thermometers. All glasses take a slight permanent set up to a certain point under continual pressure, and this tends to diminish the capacity of the bulb of a newly-made thermometer, making the instrument read higher than formerly, if it was graduated when newly made. Herr Schott says that this change, which may be considered as flow or non-elasticity, is generally least when the glass contains only one base, but, ordinarily, glasses containing but one base have a considerable tendency to devitrify and have undesirable working qualities. He proposes the following as a compromise:—

Soda,	14·5
Lime,	7·0
Alumina,	2·5
Zinc Oxide,	7·0
Silica,	67·0
Boric Acid,	2·0
	100·0

This glass is said to be subject to only $\frac{1}{6}$ of the flow or non-elastic set of the soft German soda glasses and $\frac{1}{3}$ of ordinary flint-glasses.

Very fusible Enamel and other Glasses.—When the silica is still more reduced in relation to the basic constituents very easily fusible glasses are obtained. These glasses are sometimes used as vehicles for coloring material and for other purposes, as, for example, covering the platinum electrodes which have to be sealed into other glass. The highly-fusible glasses having excess of base are easily disintegrated by water and acids; indeed, in the air the surface often becomes efflorescent. The highly fusible glasses lack that viscidity which allows easy blowing into bulbs, and a mass will often burst rather than blow out, even when care is exercised; this being specially true of glasses or enamels containing an excess of lead oxide. The following two will serve as examples:—

Highly-fusible medium free from lead.

Silica,	5 parts
Dried Borax,	4 ,,
Nitre,	3 ,,

Highly-fusible medium containing lead.

Silica,	5 parts
Red Lead,	4 ,,
Dried Borax,	2 ,,
Nitre,	2 ,,

The composition of the above glasses may be considerably varied without much altering the general character of the glass, and, as before indicated, the quality of fusibility is completely under control, as we have a complete range between the highly refractory silica, and the last mentioned media which completely fuse at a low red heat. In another chapter will be found instructions for the preparation of glass on a small scale,

Glass Tubing and Rods.—Although, as will be explained farther on, glass, as scraps or in any other form, may be worked into shape before the blowpipe, it is a matter of general convenience to obtain glass intended for blowpipe work either in the form of rods or tubes, as the making of these is a very inexpensive operation at the glass-house (for the method of making, see p. 131). Putting aside special colored or fancy materials, the commercial glass tubing and rod ordinarily obtainable from dealers in chemical apparatus consists of three kinds. Hard Bohemian tubing, which is so infusible as to be worked with difficulty, is scarcely used, except for chemical operations at a red heat, and it has quite a secondary interest from the glass-blowing point of view. For ordinary work, the choice lies between the soft German or Thuringian soda-glass and the so-called flint-glass, having lead as a characteristic constituent; this flint-glass containing sometimes potash and sometimes soda as its alkali. The respective advantages and disadvantages of these two glasses are as follows:—

German Soda-Glass can be worked in any part of the flame, or even in a bad and ragged flame, without becoming discolored, but requires more careful annealing than flint-glass, is far more liable to disintegration or devitrification than flint-glass, and specimens of slightly-different composition do not work so well together as slightly-different specimens of flint-glass. Old stock of soft German glass is often unworkable by reason of its disintegrated condition, and even the most experienced person may fail to detect this state in purchasing the glass.

Flint-Glass or Lead-Glass.—This glass is blackened by the reduction of lead to the metallic state, if the blowpipe flame is unsatisfactory by reason of imperfect combustion; but to the expert worker this is no disadvantage. To the beginner this blackening is perhaps an advantage, as it forces him to work with a flame in which the combustion is complete,—the flame which is hottest and best for all kinds of glass. As far as I know, flint-glass does not essentially deteriorate by age, although the surface may become corroded. Flint-glass tubing, with an inconvenient tendency to devitrify, is sometimes, but very seldom, met with, although all flint-glass, if the surface is alternately oxidised and reduced, undergoes a surface change, the nature of which I believe has not hitherto been recognised, but which I deal with in another place (p. 196). Flint-glass can be safely heated and cooled more rapidly than German soda-glass, requires less careful annealing, and subject to any operative difficulty, on account of varying fusibility, all ordinary samples of flint-glass may be worked together and joined. Considering all things, I prefer flint-glass for general work and as a material for beginners.

Gauging and Nomenclature of Rods and Tubing.—Glass rods and tubing, from the nature of the method adopted in the manufacture, cannot be made to an exact size, and every length must necessarily be varying in diameter, although the lack of uniformity may be very slight for a short length. Attempts have been made to indicate frequently occurring sizes by purely arbitrary numbers, but such proposals have failed completely, and must do so, as each constructor of a scale tends to start with the size he uses most frequently, as No. 1. Two scales of numbers now before me, arranged from the point of use in the chemical laboratory, agree in taking as No. 1 a size a trifle under $\frac{1}{4}$ of an inch in diameter, as ordinarily used for the tubes of wash bottles and gas flasks, the size most frequently used, but after this there is practically no agreement; No. 19 on one scale being a size suited for making sprengel pumps, and a trifle over $\frac{1}{4}$ of an inch in diameter; while No. 19 on the other scale is a thin-walled tube of over an inch in diameter. In workshops where current articles are made, sizes of tubes are commonly known by their uses, and a somewhat similar system prevails in chemical laboratories where "sprengel" tubing means the size ordinarily used in making mercurial pumps. Special names of this kind will be always used, whatever system of gauging is employed, but I would urge the desirability of discarding all random nomenclature by arbitrary numbers, and the employment of a simple system in which two numbers give the outside and inside diameters. For this purpose the millimetre is very convenient, and the numbers indicating the two diameters can be written in succession, with a rule or minus sign between them; thus, 25-19, which would mean a tube 25 millimetres outside diameter and 19 millimetres in the bore, giving a side 3 millimetres thick.

The millimetre unit is very convenient, in so much that, except in the case of tubes used for thermometers, a fraction of a millimetre need seldom be used, and in addition it will be quite accurate enough for ordinary purposes if the millimetre is regarded as the twenty-fifth of an inch,—so the figures and the system of gauging now suggested may be looked upon as either millimetres or as twenty-fifths of an inch. In fig. 55, sizes of glass tubing and rod convenient for general work are shown, and putting aside flat-bore thermometer tubing and flat tubing generally, the sizes shown will sufficiently provide for the ordinary needs of glass-blowing operations,—at any rate this selection will serve a beginner. Under each figure is indicated its gauge numbers on the millimetre or inch twenty-fifth standard (fig. 55), and for miscellaneous work the sizes most used are 7-5 and 15-12. These suggestions, as to generally useful sizes, must be taken merely as a rough guide to making a generally useful selection from the stock of the dealer, but if a greater variety is selected, a few lengths of heavy tubing bordering on 17-11 may be added, as, by softening these and drawing out, considerable variety can be obtained. In selecting tubes, canes which are straight, free from nodulous projections, round, equal in thickness of the side, and fairly parallel throughout the length, should be chosen. Some tubes have minute bores in the wall, these arising from bubbles and the original mass from

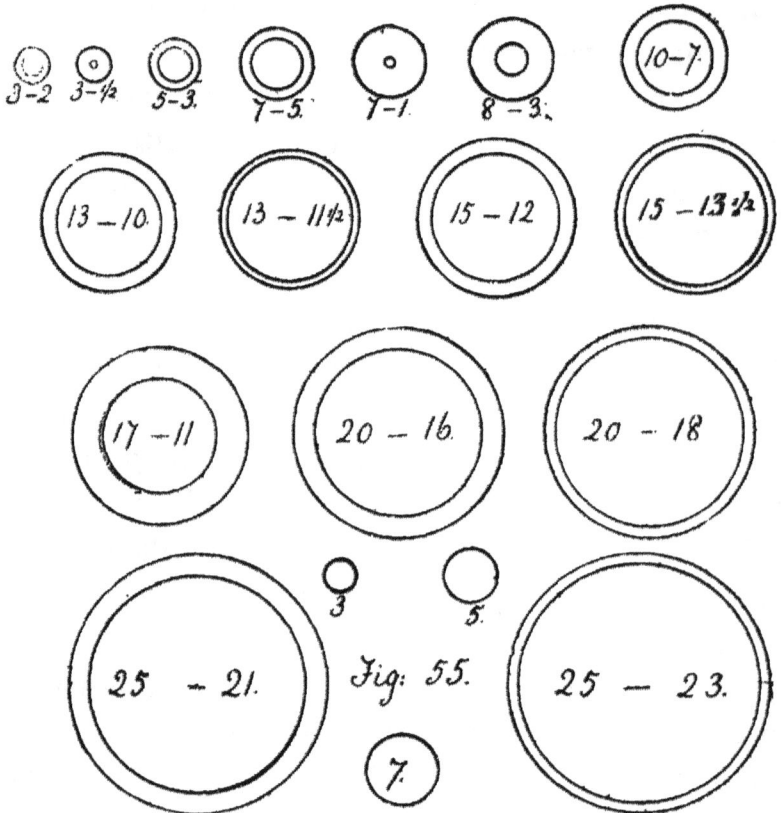

Fig. 55.

which the tube was made. Such tubes should be avoided. When tube has to be selected between certain limits of size, set gauges like fig. 47, D and E, are often useful; these being of thin sheet-metal.

Gauging Flat Tubes and Flat-bore Thermometer Tubes.—Flat tubes are now rather largely used for making the bulbs of such hydrometers as are required to float between the plates of secondary batteries and for some other purposes, while flat-bore tubes are now almost universal for mercurial thermometers. Flat rods are used in laboratories, and are very convenient for certain classes of work, as a flat rod also serves to some extent as a spatula. Two measurements at right angles may serve very well in the case of flat tubes, flat rods, or thermometer tubes, although the exact shape of the section is not indicated in this way. As the two

Fig. 56.

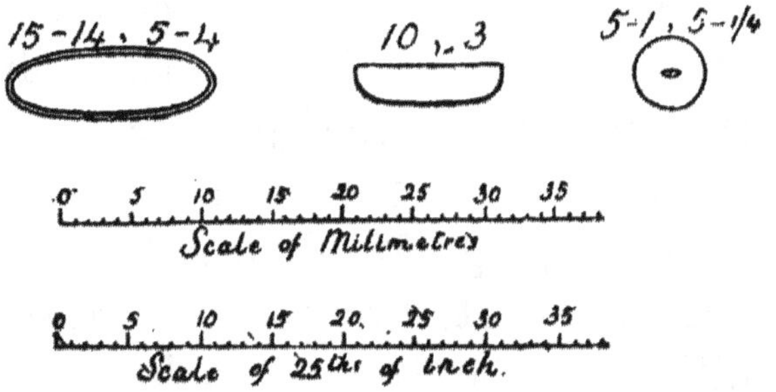
15-14, 5-4
10, 3
5-1, 5-1/4
0 5 10 15 20 25 30 35
Scale of Millimetres
0 5 10 15 20 25 30 35
Scale of 25ths of inch.

diameters of a round tube are indicated by figures separated by a minus sign, it is convenient to employ a comma to distinguish between the cross measurements of a flat rod or tube. This is sufficiently illustrated by fig. 56. The measurements of ordinary rods and tubes can be taken with such callipers as are shown in fig. 47, and then read off on a divided scale; but, in the case of thermometer tubing, a direct reading can be taken from the end of the tube over which a stage micrometer is laid, a hand lens being, of course, necessary in ordinary cases. An obvious precaution is to turn the engraved side of the stage micrometer towards the tube.

Cleaning Glass Tubes.—Tubing for making thermometers is usually closed at the ends when first made, so dirt is excluded and special cleaning is not necessary; and a similar course is often adopted in the case of tubing intended for making barometers. The bulk of the glass tubing is, however, sent out with open ends, and has become dirty inside before it reaches the user. In many cases it is sufficient to push in a lightly-fitting plug of blotting-paper or rag; push this as far as it will go with the jumper, fig. 52, A; then, holding the tube vertically, dance the jumper up and down until the plug is driven through. In other cases the wire bodkin, fig. 52, B, can be used to draw a strip of rag, tufted at the end, through the tube. If the condition of the tube is such that it requires washing, a loose plug of rag may be inserted, water poured in, and the plug driven through with the jumper; the operation being repeated until all the dirt is released, when the tube may be rinsed and set on end to dry. Another convenient way of wet-scrubbing the inside is to tie a tuft of cloth in the middle of a string rather more than twice the length of the tube, and after having drawn one end of the string through, the tuft is pulled backwards and forwards. It is very seldom that acids or alkaline solutions are required in cleaning glass tubes, and they should be avoided. For the complete drying of the inside of a tube, the tube should be warmed, and air passed through it from the bellows or *sucked* through it by the mouth, a length of rubber tube being used as a mouthpiece. For wiping the dust from short lengths of tube the small brushes sold for cleaning tobacco-pipes may be used, but the hard iron wire is liable to rift the inside of the tube and cause it to break. The inside of a glass tube——especially of a tube which is very thick——is very sensitive to abrasion, and if the inside is slightly scratched the tube is liable to break spontaneously soon after; hence the use of copper for the jumper and the wire bodkin. Perhaps the most fatal cleaning rod is cane, the silicious coating of which will almost certainly scratch the inside and cause the tube to break.

CHAPTER V.

THE VARIOUS METHODS OF WORKING AND BLOWING GLASS. DIVISION BY RIFTING. ABRASION. SHEARING AND SHANKING. DRILLING. GLASS IN THE BLOWPIPE FLAME: GENERAL CONDITIONS AND PRECAUTIONS. MOUTHING. DRAWING OUT. SEALING. BULBS. PERFORATION OF THE HOT GLASS. BENDING. JOINING AND BRANCHING. AIR TRAPPING AND INSIDE JOINS. HANDLES AND RINGS. GRADUATION. ETCHING. ANNEALING, ETC., ETC.

Characteristic Methods of Working.—These depend mainly on the fact of glass being highly elastic, brittle, and badly conductive of heat at ordinary temperatures, while at higher temperatures it is remarkably tough—almost like leather—and at a still higher heat it becomes viscous and semi-fluid like thick treacle. Yet more strongly heated it becomes almost, or quite, fluid.

Cutting or Dividing Rods or Tubes.—The method of dividing a tube or rod by making a file scratch across it, and then straining with the hands as if one were striving to bend the tube and bring the file scratch on the outer curve—for the position of the hands see fig. 57—is very well known, and for tubes or rods up to about 18 mm. (or $\frac{18}{25}$ of an inch) it is fairly satisfactory when the wall of the tube is

CUTTING TUBES.

rather thick in proportion. The grinding of one face of the file, to renew the edge, has been already

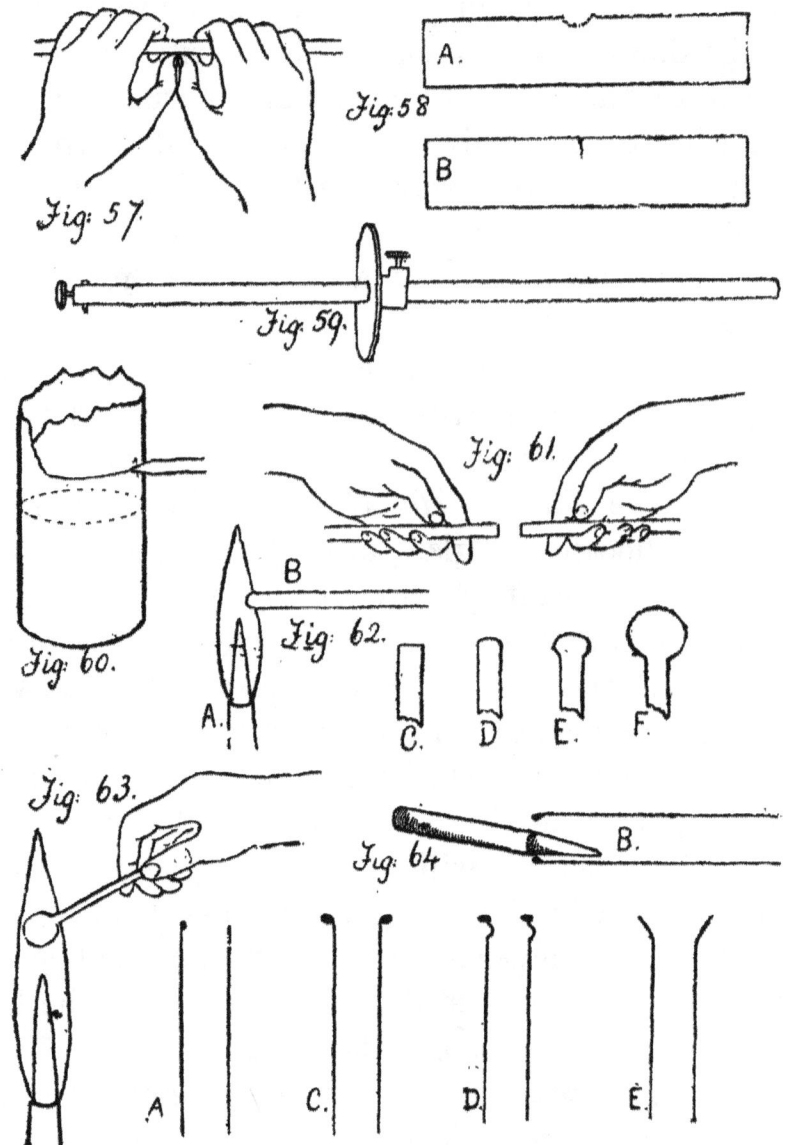

mentioned (p. 53). No invariable rule as to the degree of pressure with the file, or the speed of its motion across the glass, can be given, as the action of the file in this case appears to depend upon the accident of some rough particle upon it producing a true rift like a diamond cut; but this rift can seldom be seen, as the general scratch or abrasion conceals it. Either of the knives already described (p. 53) will give a cleaner cut than the file,—that is to say, less of the scratch element; yet the file has several considerable advantages as a single tool for many uses, as it may become a basis for other methods. One advantage of the file is that it can be used on hot glass,—that is to say, glass which has cooled so far as to be just bordering upon the viscous state.

Use of the File on Hot Glass.—When a division has to be effected on glass already hot, the file may be used very advantageously at the stage indicated above. Resting the glass on the edge of the table, the edge of the file is drawn across, backwards and forwards, slowly and with rather considerable pressure. A rift will be formed which will generally go, of itself, all round, or so nearly round that a slight blow with the handle of the file will separate the glass. When the file is used in this way on hot glass I have not found that the temper of the file suffers if it is kept in motion on the glass; still, the cold file on the hot glass may be a little more efficient if the edge of the file is drawn across a damp sponge before use, as then a trace of water lodges in the roughnesses of the cutting edge, and this may be a protection. The more keen-edged knives, described in the chapter on tools, and again referred to below, must not be used on hot glass, or the edge would certainly lose its hardness.

The Difference between a Scratch and a Rift or Cut: the Use of the Glazier's Diamond.—Although the glazier's diamond is scarcely ever used by glass-blowers in the ordinary course of their work, it is often useful in cutting colored sheet glasses into strips for ready balling or massing in the flame; but, apart from this, a study of the use of the diamond should give a clear understanding of the nature of all those methods of separation in which a crack or rift is concerned. When a broken splinter of diamond, mounted pencil fashion—the ordinary writing diamond—is drawn over a surface of glass, a rough groove is ploughed out, and a section of this groove, magnified, will look something like fig. 58, A. In spite of this, there is usually no true rift of the nature of a crack. When, however, the edge of a suitable crystal of natural diamond is drawn over the surface of a glass plate at the correct angle, the smooth edge of the diamond slides over the surface of the glass, and the glass is so strained by the pressure concentrated on a very narrow line that it cracks or rifts, as suggested, but exaggerated by the supposed section B, fig. 58, and if a bending strain is put on the glass the crack extends and the plate separates. Sometimes a cutting diamond not only gives a true cut, but also crushes down the surface of the glass, and a diamond of this kind is called a rough cutting diamond. The rough portion of the rough cut, however, has but little in common with the scratch of the writing diamond. Cutting glass tubes or rods by the file scratch is (except in the case of the hot glass and the cold file) a more or less fortuitous process. More certain in their action are the

Glass-Workers' Knives.—These have been described (p. 53), and it only remains to indicate the method of use. In each case the knife is held in the right hand, so that its plane is vertical, and the cutting edge upwards. The tube is now held across the edge, held down with the thumb, and rotated. A cut from $\frac{1}{6}$ to $\frac{1}{4}$ of the way round is generally sufficient in the case of tubes up to about 18 mm. (or $\frac{18}{25}$ of an inch), when the separation may generally be effected as shown by fig. 57. When, however, special heating methods are to be adopted to bring about separation, it is generally desirable to take the cut all the way round, taking care that the ends exactly meet.

Expedients to facilitate Separation.—When a tube which has been cut by the file or knife fails to separate by a gentle strain, as shown in fig. 57, various expedients may be adopted, but no one can be mentioned as infallible in all cases. The most useful are the following:—

The Bead of Hot Glass.—If a small bead or globule of very hot glass is suddenly brought down on the file or knife mark, a crack or rift will often pass quite uniformly round the tube, and separation will be effected. The common recommendation (in books on chemical laboratory manipulation) to melt up the bead on a thin thread of glass is not a method to follow, as one gets no satisfactory push down of the bead into the crack. It is far more satisfactory to melt a globule of glass on the end of a rod of 2 or 3 mm. in diameter. If a tube is unequally annealed, the crack will not pass round uniformly, in which case one of the following methods may be adopted.

The Hot Half-Ring.—A file or knife cut is made all round the tube, and one of the half-rings (fig. 42 and p. 54) of suitable size, being made red hot, is fixed in a small vice. The tube being now taken by both hands, is rotated slowly in the half-ring, care being taken to keep the cut in correspondence with the half-ring.

The Hot Platinum Wire.—Where electric current is available, this method may sometimes prove convenient if many articles are to be treated in succession. A wire of suitable length and diameter for the current is turned once round the tube, a scale of talc being laid between, where the wire returns upon itself; after which the current is passed, so as to heat the wire to redness.

The Pointed Flame Method.—This is, perhaps, on the whole, the most convenient, if the bead or globule of hot glass proves unsatisfactory or fails. The file or knife cut is made all round the tube, and close on

F

each side of it there is wrapped round the tube a strip of moist blotting-paper; these strips being bound on with thread, the tube is now very quickly rotated some little distance in front of a very small and pointed blowpipe flame. The space between the strips of blotting-paper may be from $\frac{1}{16}$ of an inch to $\frac{1}{8}$ of an inch.

The Glazier's Diamond.—When this is used in cutting glass tubes (and engineers use it to cut their water gauge tubes to length), the inside of the tube is always cut. The diamond is set in a small projection on a brass or copper rod, a sliding stop serving as a guide in cutting round. Fig. 59 shows the arrangement, which may also serve for splitting a piece of tube longitudinally to make a sheet of glass, by softening and opening out.

Dividing Tubes or Rods by Grinding.—Thick heavy rods of about an inch in diameter, and tubes of similar or rather less diameter, and exceptionally thick in the walls—let us suppose a tube of 15–3 mm. (see gauge system, p. 74)—are those which are most uncertain in cutting off by the above methods; and if much work has been done on such a tube, or cutting in an exact place is important, it is often better to divide the tube by a sawing or grinding action, using the circular lap, fig. 53, C, fed with emery and oil, or to adopt one of the abrasion methods described a little farther on.

Trimming Irregular Edges to Shape.—One of the most generally convenient ways is to warm the glass before the blowpipe until it is soft, and then trim the soft glass with fine pointed scissors. Care should be taken not to put the scissors in the blowpipe flame.

Leading a Crack.—In the case of fairly well annealed glass of uniform thickness, this can be done with very great rapidity and facility, the crack following a red hot wire, a glowing pastile, or a minute flame held a little in advance of the end of the crack. Fig. 60 indicates the way of working, whether the charcoal sticks (p. 56), the minute flame (p. 56), or a hot wire is used. A line is drawn round the tube or bulb with ink, this line being conveniently about $\frac{1}{16}$ of an inch from the route of the proposed crack. The crack must be led down from an existing crack, or a crack may be established near the edge by making a file mark and heating with wire, pastile, or flame. The crack is led down so as to enter the proposed route at an angle of about 45°, and then brought round as indicated by the figure.

Trimming by Crushing or Shanking.—This is done with the optical shanks, fig. 50, A, or the rather fine pointed pliers, fig. 50, B. The main point to attend to is to grip very little of the glass at a time, and to hold the glass close up to the part to be crushed, so as to minimise vibration.

Filing and Grinding Glass.—If a common file is kept thoroughly wet with oil of turpentine, in which camphor has been dissolved to saturation, the softer kinds of glass may be filed almost as easily as brass is ordinarily filed. The use of type metal and other laps with emery and oil has already been sufficiently indicated. A saw with a plain copper blade may be used with the same mixture, and a bow saw with a copper wire as a blade may also be used. With each tool the great point of success is to press lightly and ease back frequently for the cutting mixture to come forward. An old American "star" hack saw, the teeth of which have been singly crushed off by sharp blows with a hammer, the tooth being laid on the edge of a steel stake, makes a useful tool for sawing glass if kept well wetted with the solution of camphor in turpentine. I have found the "star" hack saws to differ somewhat in hardness, and only those so hard that each individual tooth can be rather crushed than knocked off are specially suitable for glass.

Drilling Small Holes ; Cutting Large Holes.—If a steel drill, made to a rather long spear-like point and hardened to the extreme, is used with the above-mentioned solution of camphor in oil of turpentine, very quick progress can be made. There is no special advantage with the old-fashioned glass drill stock, and nothing is more convenient than the small American drill stock with bevel gear, but the pressure on the drill must be light, the work must be kept flooded with the turpentine and camphor mixture, and the drill should be eased back frequently. A broken end of very hard steel is as good as the formed drill when the work is once started, and can be renewed by beating off a little from the end. As the drill should be so hard as to be easily crushed by a blow with the hammer, the renewing of the end is easy if the extreme end—say $\frac{1}{16}$ of an inch—is laid on an anvil and crushed by a sharp blow. In cutting out a large hole—for example, a hole from $\frac{1}{4}$ of an inch in diameter to an inch or more—the usual method is to use the end of a copper tube charged with emery and oil and turned in the lathe; light pressure and frequent easing back being desirable. The end of the copper tube can be kept in place for starting by a guide piece of cardboard, which may be a disc glued on, the disc, of course, fitting the inside of the copper tube, or a piece of cardboard with a perforation corresponding to the outside of the copper tube. This cardboard is either clamped or glued on. The best precaution against fracture, when the tube breaks through the other side, is a thick sheet of soft rubber next the glass, this being backed up by a flat board—but gentle pressure against the cutting tube is to be understood as essential. Rejecting the very soft copper, we may go to hard steel, as tubes of high tool steel can now be obtained. The end of the steel tube must be tempered fully hard, and then crushed all round with a hammer, by the method suggested above in the case of the "star" hack saw on the one hand, and the broken-end drill on the other hand. The general manipulations are as with the copper tube, and the broken edge of the steel tube can be renewed by crushing with the hammer.

Polishing.—After the various abrasive or grinding operations a partial polishing may be required. The finest flour emery mixed with oil and spread on a revolving lap or a plate of type metal can be a first step, and putty powder (stannic oxide), similarly used, a second and final step, for obtaining such polish as is likely to be required.

Lenses.—Anything like full details as to the making of lenses is outside the scope of the present work, but a reader who has either made a mass of special glass, by methods indicated farther on, or who wishes to make a lens, will have but little difficulty in roughly forming it by attention to the following particulars. The curve determined upon is stuck with compasses on a sheet of brass and two corresponding templets are made: one, a templet for the inside of the curve, and the other for the outside. These form the guides in turning two metal moulds or shaping tools: one concave and the other convex; and for a single lens or occasional work these may be of type metal. A piece of glass being "shanked" (see p. 85) roughly to a circle is cemented with pitch to a flanged wooden handle and is ground against one of these moulds, which must be freely supplied with emery and paraffin oil—coarse at first; the great point being to so systematically change the position and so alternate with cross strokes that there is no working up to a centre. After the first rough grinding the mould or tool must be turned afresh to the templet, and so after each successive grinding, with finer emery each time, until the finest flour emery of commerce is reached. The last emery should be extra fine and free from grit, obtained by washing out or elutriating the finest from a commercial sample. The polishing may be with elutriated putty powder on a piece of thin chamois leather laid on the once more corrected mould. If a thin knife is introduced into the pitch under the edge of the glass, a sharp blow on an opposite point against the table will detach the glass from the pitch, when the other side may be worked to a similar or to another curve. The above particulars only very partially represent the usages of an optical workshop, but I give them as indicating the readiest means I know of by which a beginner, left to his own resources, may construct a lens. In the next chapter will be found mention of lenses formed by melting glass in a ring of platinum wire; also hollow lenses of a still rougher kind, but useful for certain demonstrative purposes.

Glass in the Blowpipe Flame; Fundamental Considerations.—The first tendency of a mass of glass presented to the flame is to crack, owing to the expansion of the surface, while the mass is still brittle. To avoid fracture in heating, the heating should be slow and uniform, especially when the glass is thick or of irregular shape. Glasses vary very much as regards their tendency to break under heat, not only on account of the material of the glass but also of the annealing. Those who have been accustomed only to work small and thin-walled tubes will be surprised at the time required to safely heat through a thick tube about 17–11 mm., (see p. 74 and fig. 55), even when the tube is of well annealed soft flint glass.

Precautions in First Heating. — It is a very common practice to warm the tube or other glass in the smoky flame of the lamp first, the tube being turned round on its axis continually, so that a certain length of the tube shall be warmed uniformly all round. When the soot first deposited on the glass begins to burn off the blowpipe flame may be used; the best position being about the middle of the solid front of the flame, as indicated by fig. 9, C. Tubes of very thin glass or tubes of very small diameter may be placed almost at once in the hottest part of the flame, and many workers prefer to give the preliminary warming at some distance in front of the blowpipe flame rather than by means of the smoky flame. When several articles of the same kind are to be made of very thick tube it is often possible to economise time by placing the pieces into an annealing tube or oven (fig. 54, A and B) to warm. Sometimes a crack occurs in heating, which crack is subsequently melted up and healed in everything except that a faint indication is left on the finished article. A heat crack of this kind is practically no disadvantage. At this stage the pupil must learn the art of

Turning the Piece uniformly and steadily.—This is essential for that even heating which is a prime factor in the production of uniform and symmetrical work. Until both the operation of blowing and that of constantly turning the piece held become so far reflex that they can be kept up without thought or effort, the learner makes slow progress. The usual mode of turning is by resting the rod or tube in a hollow, formed by bending the first and second finger and turning it round by means of the thumb; the third and fourth fingers being sometimes almost passive, but when the tube or rod is long and heavy they may assist both in supporting and turning. The habit of turning may be acquired by practising the turning of a pencil in each hand without break or alteration of speed while talking or reading, and finally the two pencils must be brought into line, as shown by fig. 61, the turning of both being strictly synchronous. Afterwards the same position must be practised with tubes or rods of unequal diameter. Important as the turning may be from the point of view of even heating, it is if anything more essential from the point of view of keeping a softened mass from deflecting. The mass of softened glass is never quite fluid, and the rotation gives a constant correction of the successive deflections. It may be taken as a general thing that whenever a mass of softened glass is at the end of a tube or rod, that the rod or tube must be kept rotating on its axis, unless when held in a vertical position.

Influence of Surface Tension, Gravity, and the Drift of the Flame on the Softened End of a Rod.— A first step is to melt a symmetrical ball or knob on the end of a glass rod, and in doing this count must be taken of the above three influences which are paramount in all work with softened glass. Let A, fig. 62, be a blowpipe flame, and B a sharply cut off glass rod held as shown, but steadily rotated so that the heating shall be uniform. As the glass softens, the first effect noticed is that the sharp angle disappears and becomes rounded: the section C becomes D. As the heating is continued more of the glass softens, and the rounding becomes more pronounced as at E, fig. 62. This rounding is due to the fact that the free surface of a liquid or a semi-liquid is physically of the nature of an elastic skin, which tends to compress the liquid and force it into that form in which the surface will be least in proportion to the volume of the liquid. When the growing ball of softened glass becomes considerably larger in proportion than E, the influence of gravity upon it will become very apparent; a rate of turning which was sufficient before now becomes insufficient to prevent the softened mass of glass falling down by gravity, and it becomes necessary to turn the softened end of the rod a little upwards, if the globule of glass is to be kept in symmetry with the stem. The drift of the blast also tells, and the softened end must also be directed a little towards the jet, but a time is reached at which the globule is so large that, turn as quickly as one will, and adjust as carefully as may be against gravity and the blast of the blowpipe, it cannot be kept symmetrical on the stem. A larger globule in proportion to the stem than that shown at F can scarcely be obtained by the most skilful worker, and when such a globule is of unsoiled glass and successful it has almost the surface of a lens. Fig. 63 shows a position of flame, hand, and glass at the last stage of making such a globule: but it will be obvious from what has been said that the exact adjustment will vary in each individual case. On removing the globule from the blowpipe the rotation must be continued until the globule has somewhat set. The student who can make such globules with certainty has learned to master the most important influence, and has made no mean progress.

Rounding, spreading out, or contracting the Mouth of a Tube.—If the end of a tube is softened by being held in the blowpipe flame, as indicated by figs. 62, B, and 63, the glass being turned meanwhile, the softened glass will tend to draw itself together by virtue of surface tension, and the mouth of the tube will be contracted internally, as shown by fig. 64, A. In order to finish with a rounded end, which shall neither be contracted nor expanded, a small rod of electric light carbon or an iron wire, which has been warmed and rubbed over with a trace of wax, is (or one of the turnpins shown by fig. 48) placed inside, as indicated at B, fig. 64, so that it bears gently against the unsoftened part. That turning of the tube on its axis, which should not have stopped, now forces out the internal welt. Afterwards, the end of the tube should be made as hot as practicable, without again softening it, in order to undo the effect of any unequal chill, strain, or abrasion by the iron; indeed, this precaution should be taken after the use of any shaping tool. It more often happens that the mouth of the tube has to be turned slightly outwards, which may be done with the carbon or wire cones or turnpins, fig. 48, A and C. When the solid cone A is used there is a tendency to push the softened glass in, so as to form a kind of welt like C, fig. 64, and if too great a length is heated the tube may become deformed, as shown at D, fig. 64; when, on the other hand, the wire cone C, fig. 48, is turned round in the softened end there is but little tendency to compress the glass, and a mouth like E, fig. 64, is the result. The wire, like all iron tools used against hot glass, should occasionally be very slightly surface charged with wax. As a mouth like fig. E is generally preferred by the public, and is less likely to break spontaneously, professional glass-blowers ordinarily employ the skeleton turnpin as shown, or its near mechanical equivalent: a blade of iron with a spear-like end. Contracting the mouth of a tube by means of a shaping tool is a much less common operation than expanding, as drawing out, and the natural falling in of the glass, are ordinarily sufficient. In some cases, as when a small tube has to be joined to a large tube, it is convenient to contract artificially, when the female turnpins, fig. 48, B and D, may be used. The skeleton form D is generally to be preferred, as with the solid form undue compression of the glass and a deformation, of a kind similar to that indicated by fig. 64, D, are likely to result. In all cases in which the blowpipe flame is directed across the mouth of a short tube of large diameter the other end should be closed; a temporary closing with a cork or a tuft of cotton wool being ordinarily sufficient. The reason of closing is merely to obstruct blasts of hot air and even flame, which might otherwise rush down the tube and become inconvenient to the worker. It may be mentioned that a carbon cone made with a polygonal section is mechanically the equivalent of the skeleton wire cone, and is in some respects more convenient.

Drawing out and thickening Tubes; small Tubes from large.—Let A, B, fig. 65, be a length of glass tube which is heated by the blowpipe flame at C, the tube being held by both hands and rotated uniformly on its axis. A, the tube, becomes soft at C, surface tension asserts itself, and, provided that no strain is put on the glass by want of correspondence between the movements of the hands, the glass will draw together at C, by such stages as D, E, and F. If at any one of these stages the tube is withdrawn from the flame, and the ends are pulled

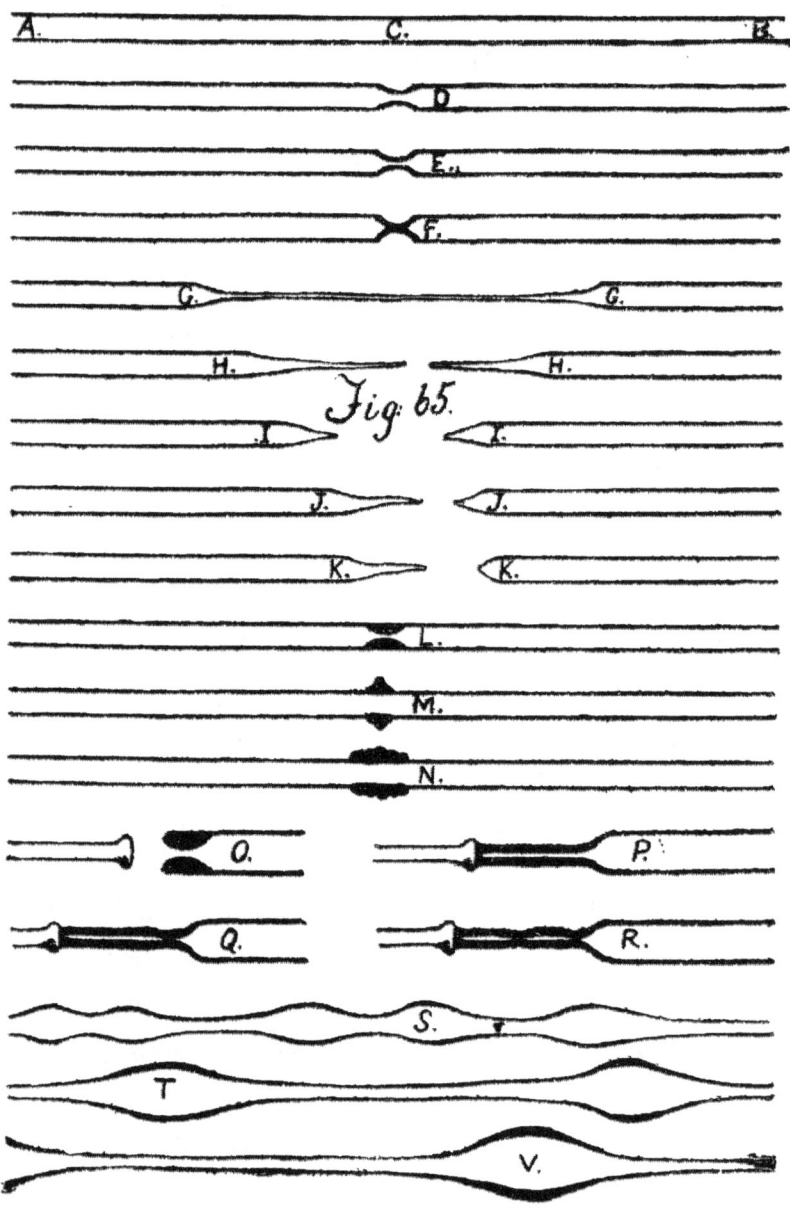

Fig. 65.

steadily and *slowly* apart, the softened portion will be drawn out to a smaller diameter: this drawn-out portion being tubular in the case of D or E, and solid in the case of F. If the ends of the tube which is softened in the middle are pulled apart *rapidly* the drawn-out portion will be very thin and thread-like in the middle. The reason of this is, that when the drawing out is rapid the softened glass has not time to cool and harden, consequently the thinnest part gives way. When, on the other hand, the drawing is slow or by stages the thinnest part loses its heat first, partially chills and becomes harder, while the thicker parts retain their heat and softness; and the next drawing out takes effect mainly on the thicker portions. This influence of the partial chilling of the thinner parts when the work is slow is a factor in many operations, and must be carefully studied. It cannot be better studied than by softening tubes and rods, and drawing out the softened portions under the following conditions : (1) slowly or by stages, after the piece is removed from the flame; the result of thus drawing out E is shown at G, the thin portion being approximately parallel; (2) rapidly, after removal from the flame, in which case E would draw out almost like H, only a long thin thread would fill the gap shown near H; (3) slowly; the piece being kept in the flame, and rotated so as to maintain the full heat of the glass. The effect of this is shown at I. In this case the thinnest part naturally becomes the hottest, but the glass separates with the formation of two little knobs as shown; (4) slowly;

the piece being kept in the flame, but the piece is so shifted that the flame plays constantly near the thick part at one end of the constricted portion. In this case one of the separated portions will be closed much more obtusely than the other, as shown at J′, and if a small flame be used, and the heat is kept well to the butt of the drawn-out part, a closing like K′ can be obtained. In all these cases, and indeed generally, it must be understood that the piece is kept rotating on its axis all the time. I will leave over K′, which represents the first stage in almost all closings of the end of a tube, and continue the consideration of drawing out. Although D, fig. 65, represents the effect of heating the tube C, if there is neither compression of the ends together nor a pulling apart, a very slight and almost imperceptible pressure together will give a gathering or thickening like L, and the pulling out of this gathering will give a fine tube much thicker in the wall than would otherwise have been obtainable: often a matter of importance. It is, however, possible to gather a considerable mass of glass by other means. If a small blowpipe flame is used, and a narrow ring round the tube is heated, gentle compression will give a gathering like M, fig. 65, and several gatherings of this kind made close together and united by cautious compression may take such a form as N. Such gatherings on a tube are useful when a very thick walled drawn-out portion is required, as in the case of the nose of an

THICKENED ENDS.

ordinary male syringe (also in the case of bulbs, to be treated of farther on). When, however, the thickened drawing out is to come at the end of a tube, as in the case of the syringe, another method is more convenient. Let O, fig. 65, be a plain tube, one end of which has been heated, the tube being held for the gathering much as is shown at fig. 63, except that the heating is more forward in the blowpipe flame and some little distance from the end of the tube; indeed, if the heating were quite at the end, a globule would be formed. When the condition shown at O, fig. 65, is reached, a heated rod is attached to the extreme end, and O is slowly drawn out to the form shown by P. Here we have the kind of thickened and drawn out end often required on a thin-walled tube, the common glass syringe being a familiar instance. In this case the end would be further shaped by local drawings, and a description of these will serve as an example. Before the end has completely chilled it is re-heated, gently drawn to the shape Q, again heated with a small flame, drawn to the form R, cut off at the narrow portion, and held for an instant in the flame to round off the sharp edge. Small tubes may very conveniently be drawn from larger tubes, and it is often more convenient to do this than to use small tubes obtained ready made from the glass-house, as larger portions may be left here and there, as required for bulbs, etc. A thick, heavy tube, about 17–11, may be heated in a large blowpipe flame, slightly thickened, and a two foot length of tube, about 3-2, drawn from it at one pull. Another similar heating will give another similar pull, end to end with the first, but with a slight expansion between them. If suitable rests are provided, almost any length of small tubing can thus be drawn in one piece from large tubing. By a careful adjustment of the position of the flame and the rate of draw, the drawing out of the small tube can be made almost continuous rather than periodic, but complete uniformity of diameter is out of the question in this process. By this method it becomes possible to draw out a tube of 30 or 40 feet long, and lay in position at the same time; for instance, a tube laid in a horizontal conduit as an insulation for a high potential wire. I failed in the corresponding operation vertically; an attempt to make and raise the tube for a water barometer at one operation. It is very convenient to draw a considerable number of various pieces from the larger tubes and to keep them ready for use, and S, T, V (fig. 65) will give a general idea of such treatment of a large tube. The advantage of making a number of such pieces rests with the fact that, by exercising care, the heat may be made to creep along the large tube without breaking it, and the whole of the length can be drawn off with only the loss of time involved in one slow heating.

Closing the End of a Tube: shaping and treating the Closed End.—Hermetically sealed Tubes.—In the previous section, K′, fig. 65 is referred to as the most ordinary kind of closing, and instructions are given for making. It generally happens that the end has to be rounded, and the first thing is to eliminate the little knob of glass or bleb which is in the centre of the seal, but, if the last draw off is made with a small pointed flame, and close to the

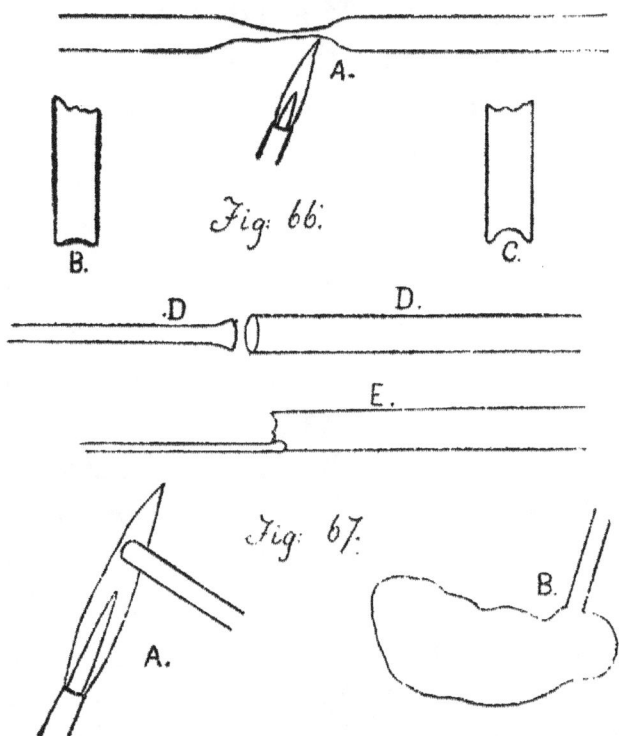

thick part, as indicated by fig. 66, A, the bleb may be very unobtrusive at the outset. To remove the bleb the bottom is well and uniformly heated in the blowpipe flame, after which the open end of the tube is gently blown into, so as to slightly expand the bottom—more, indeed, than its final expansion. After a pause of perhaps half-a-second for the thin portion to chill, the blowing is renewed, and this, the thicker bleb, tends to expand, as it remains soft. The bottom being now re-heated, the thin parts tend to become hot through first, and to thicken. When the bottom is again softened, the tube should be once more blown into gently, until the right degree of rounding is obtained. If a flat bottom is required the bleb is removed and the bottom is blown round, as above described. The bottom being now held just on the outside of the blowpipe flame and the tube rotated on its axis, the bottom will draw itself in by surface tension; but if the softened bottom is brought down gently on a fire-clay or carbon plate, a better shaped bottom will be obtained; slightly concave, like B, fig. 66. A more decidedly concave bottom, like C, fig. 66, can be produced by very slightly exhausting the air of the tube by suction at the mouth. The piece K', fig. 65, is supposed to have its closure made at a considerable distance from an end, but in practice an end often has to be closed with as little loss as possible. Let D, fig. 66, be the tube to be closed at the end, D'. The end is softened by the flame, and opposite is held a piece of waste glass, D'', one end of which is about the same diameter as the tube to be closed. When both are softened they are placed together, and D is drawn out for closing (see p. 98) as near to the end as possible. When more glass can be spared in making the closure it is a not uncommon practice to attach a handle-piece of waste glass towards the edge, as at

E, fig. 66, but this makes it more difficult than it otherwise would be to keep the closure truly centric. Sometimes a tube already closed at one end has to be sealed with a rounded closure. It is first closed in the usual way, after which the heat is maintained on the closed end until the expansion of the enclosed air gives the desired rounding. If now removed at once from the flame the tube would collapse at the end from the contraction of the enclosed air: hence, while the end is setting, it is necessary to apply a little heat to that portion of the tube adjacent to the closure; but if too much heat is thus applied, the end will naturally blow out. A tube sealed or closed at both ends is said to be hermetically sealed, in honour of the Alexandrian Hermes (Hermes Trismegistus), who was a renowned teacher of experimental science, and perhaps was the originator of the now common plan of preserving rare or perishable articles in sealed glass tubes. The Alexandrian Hermes appears to be sometimes confounded with the more ancient Egyptian Hermes of the period of Osiris and Isis. It is by no means improbable that articles were sealed hermetically in glass tubes, for their more effectual preservation, before the end of the third century. There is a sealed tube in the reliquary of Notre Dame at Paris, and said to contain a piece of the true Cross, and it is by no means improbable that it was first sealed before the conversion of Constantine (*circa* 310), as much of the Roman Catacomb glass, bearing Christian symbols and undoubtedly earlier than this period, is of similar character. The sealed tube of St Maurice in the Valais, which contains a thorn—said to be a thorn from the Holy Crown—is probably very much later (see p. 137 of Mr Wallace-Dunlop's *Glass in the Old World*). In the next chapter will be found some details as to sealed tubes for laboratory work and for the preservation of historical or other specimens.

The Blowing of Bulbs: Fundamental Considerations.—The blowing of a symmetrical bulb of glass, by forcing air into a soft mass, is performed under such various conditions as to necessitate several sub-headings; but the fundamental points upon which success depends may form an introduction. There are: 1st, An original mass, which is fairly symmetrical; 2nd, That this mass should be equally heated; 3rd, That the influence of gravity, if not eliminated by turning the piece, should act in the direction of the axis of the blowing tube; 4th, That the blowing be not so sudden and energetic as to continue to act on the thinnest part, which would otherwise blow out and burst. Blowing must be slow or periodic, so as to allow any unduly expanded (or thin) portions to chill, and the rest to come up with such portions.

Ordinary case of a Bulb at the end of a Tube. Such a bulb is a good starting-point for practice and study. Take a tube about 10–7 (mm. or 25th of an inch, as explained on p. 74). Close one end like K′, fig. 65 (see p. 100), and eliminate the bleb, as explained on p. 101. The glass, being now warmed gradually, is held obliquely in the flame, as shown at fig. 67, A, taking care not only to rotate steadily on the axis of the tube, but also to rotate so that the end of the piece retains its position in relation to the flame. As the glass softens the softened end may be inclined upwards, so that the glass tends to fall upon itself and thicken by gravity, or the softened part may be allowed to hang down and to extend itself; the former if a rather small and thick bulb is required, and the latter if a large and thin bulb is wanted. The beginner, at any rate, had better hold the tube with the softened part hanging down vertically when blowing, but the turning must be continued; and if a side set has been given to the soft part in bringing the tube to the vertical position, a momentary inclination must be given to the tube to set matters right. The first impulse of blowing may be given while the mass is very soft, and impulse after impulse given as the glass expands, until towards the end the greatest pressure which the lungs can exert may be employed. The result should be a bulb almost as symmetrical and true as if turned. If the hot mass had been blown with full force at first, the thinnest part of the wall, retaining its original softness, would have been chiefly expanded, and a curiously-shaped bulb, somewhat like B, fig. 67, would have resulted, the thin part, B', being so thin as to burst by the force of the breath, and showing interference colors. The bulb as first blown may not be of the right size, in which case it must be reduced or expanded. For this purpose it must be re-heated, and special care must be taken to re-heat uniformly, in which case the softened bulb will contract by surface tension without much loss of symmetry; but, if it shows signs of falling into folds, an occasional slight expansion by very gentle blowing will keep matters right. When sufficiently contracted and uniformly heated it is again blown out. The tube upon which the bulb is blown should, where practicable, be of such a length as to allow of distinct vision; and, when bulbs are to be made to a given size, a pattern bulb may be supported in a convenient position. A couple of sheet metal gauges, fig. 47, E, are useful; one gauging the limit as to largeness and the other as to smallness. Although the beginner is recommended to hold his tube with the softened end downwards when blowing, he will soon learn to blow bulbs with the tube extended horizontally, or inclining a little upwards or downwards, the axial position of the softened mass and of the bulb then depending altogether on the maintenance of the rotation.

Blowing a Bulb from a Globule of Glass.—If, instead of heating a glass rod in the way described on p. 92 and represented by fig. 62, B, a glass tube is similarly heated, a globule of glass can be made to gather at the end, and this makes in many respects a better starting-point for a bulb than does the softened end of a tube in which some of the original tube form is preserved. The bulb blown from the globule naturally has no bleb.

A Bulb from Scrap Glass or Rod.—The globule method is very useful if it is wished to blow a bulb of a foreign glass at the end of a tube—the black bulb of Daniell's hygrometer for instance. The scraps of glass may be laid one by one on the softened end of the tube with the corn tongs, and by carefully adjusting the position the heat may be made to play almost exclusively on the added glass. In a similar way a globule may be built up on the end of a tube from a rod.

Blowing a Bulb on the end of a Rod.— The following method is sometimes convenient, and great variety of shape and style can be obtained by its adoption:—A globule, as shown at fig. 62, F, is made at the end of a rod, and while it is at a full heat, a tube, A, fig. 68, also softened in the flame, is joined to it, the open end of A being brought to the mouth, and blowing is performed with the precautions already detailed. If the rod and the tube are slightly pressed together during the blowing, a form like C will be obtained, but if drawn apart during the blowing elongated bulbs with tubular tails ranging from D to E are obtained, the form E cut off at F making a pipette. Obviously, any one of the bulbs can be melted off from the rod at the narrow part and be re-blown to any desired shape.

The above method does not answer very well if the tube A, fig. 68, is very small in diameter, as the heated end joined to the soft mass often becomes deformed. When a bulb with a small stem

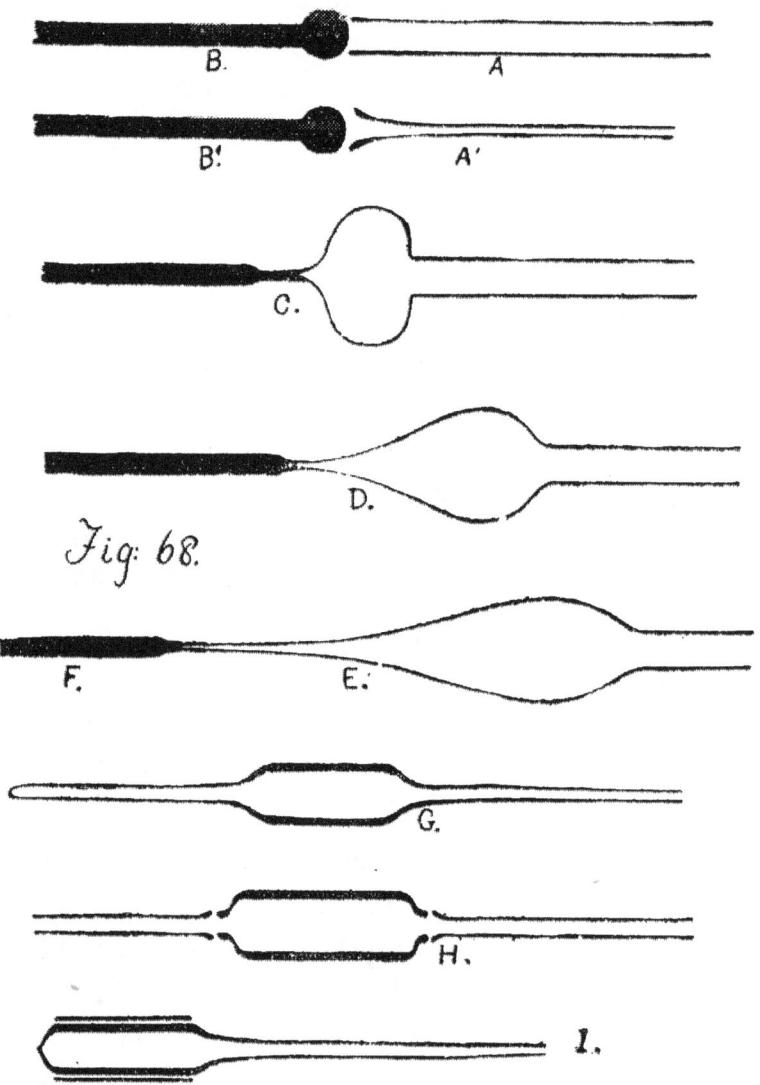

Fig. 68.

is required, a piece like A, obtained by drawing from a larger tube, is desirable. The thick mouth gives a good hold on the molten globule.

Bulbs on the Course or Length of a Tube.—One end of the tube is closed and that part on which the bulb is to be blown is uniformly heated, after which the tube is brought to the mouth by the two hands, care being taken not to stretch the soft part, and the bulb is blown in the ordinary way. The part to be expanded may be thickened, as described on p. 98 and shown by fig. 65, L and N; but if a large bulb is required between small shafts it is generally much better to draw the small shafts from a large tube and leave a portion of the original tube as a basis for the bulb. The drawing out is described on p. 97, and fig. 68, G, shows the kind of drawing out which is suitable. When it is necessary to have straight and thin shafts, longer and more parallel than can conveniently be drawn from the large tube, joining becomes necessary, the pieces being as shown at H, fig. 68. Joining is described on p. 120.

Large Bulbs.—When a very large bulb is required, it is generally much better to make it from a piece of thick walled tube, 17–11 for instance, or larger, than to thicken up, but in exceptional cases an outer sleeve may be laid on and allowed to incorporate itself with the rest. This arrangement for a large bulb at the end of a small tube is sufficiently indicated by I, fig. 68. When large bulbs are to be made, the radiator, fig. 45, is very useful. It should be placed about $\frac{1}{2}$ an inch beyond the point of the flame.

The Sleeve Method for small Bulbs.—The method of thickening by a sleeve piece is very convenient for quickly making small stout bulbs—say, about an inch in diameter, on a narrow stem, when many similar bulbs have to be made, as the sleeves can be kept hot over a burner, and no time need be lost in the preliminary heating. After what has been said, the stages of this work can be better represented diagramatically than by words. Fig. 69 shows the stages in progress. This method gives no bleb if the blowing is at the right stage.

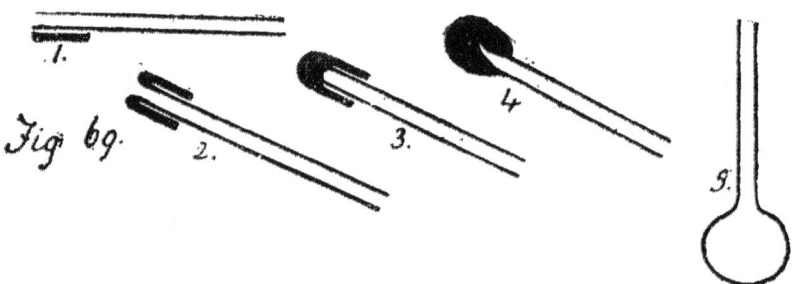

Bulbs on Tubes of fine Bore. Thermometer Tubes.—In making a bulb on a thermometer tube of small bore, whether at the end or in the course of the length, it is generally advisable to use an elastic pear or bottle for blowing, and put on a very slight pressure during the early stages of the softening, as otherwise the bore may so melt up that it becomes difficult to make a commencement of the expansion.

Distribution of Glass in the Bulb.—This will necessarily vary according to the purpose for which the bulb is intended, and in most cases it is very much under control. Let me take as a starting point a piece of thick tube drawn out with a fine stem at one end and closed at the other end, like fig. 70, A. If the heating is directed mainly on the extreme half of the large portion, the tendency will be to give a bulb thick on the shoulder, like B, while more equal heating will give a fairly uniform thickness as shown at C; and heating which tends rather away from the end will give a bulb thick in the bottom, as shown at D.

The Shape of Bulbs, and Shaping them afterwards.—The shape of a bulb is largely under control in the first instance, and by subsequent treatment the most surprising modifications can be effected by a skilled artist, including minutely modelled figures in resemblance of animals. At this stage I will merely indicate a few general methods. A bulb blown between two holding pieces, like fig. 68, C, D, or E, may be made short and turnip-like, or long, as explained on p. 107, and illustrated by fig. 68, C, D, and E, and the pear-shaped form is determined by the greater softness of one end. If the bulb is blown from a hollow original this may result from nursing the heat to one end, but in the case of D and E, the origin of the pear shape is to be found in the fact that one end is attached to a considerably softened rod, and the other to a tube of rather large diameter and scarcely softened. The control over the shape of bulb blown at the end of a tube is not

112 MODIFIED BULBS.

quite so simple, but it is easy. Take the case of fig. 70. If, instead of the globular form C, it is desired to make a long form, the piece may be

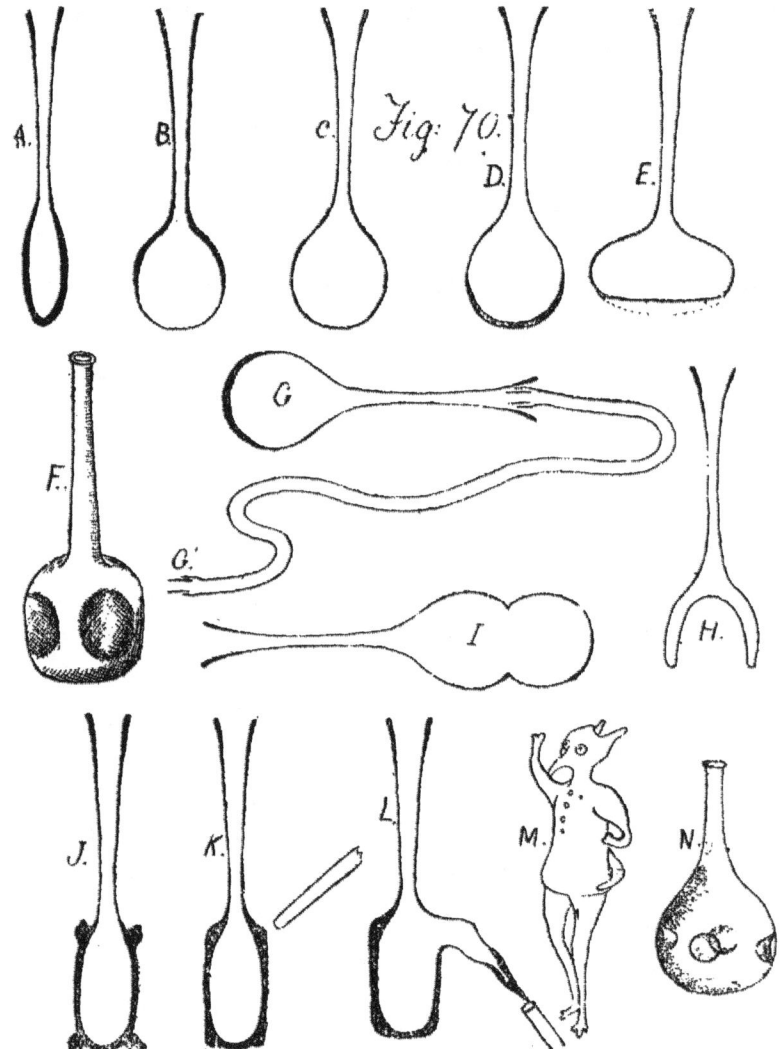

extended by swinging, between the blowings. If a more flattened form is wanted, any desired flattening is obtainable by bringing a piece of tile under the bulb just as the final expansion is given; the piece must, of course, hang vertically in this case. The effect is shown in fig. 70, E, and a re-heating of the flattened bottom followed by gentle air pressure will give such a shape as is indicated by the dotted lines, E, fig. 70.

Examples of very simple modelling on the bulb, are such operations as softening the bottom, bringing it down upon a slab of fire-clay, then merely by the softening action of the blowpipe flame, making four flats on the side. The neck being now turned out, as explained on p. 93, we have a bottle, fig. 70, F, a very ancient style indeed. For more elaborate modelling on the bulb and making the point of the blowpipe flame a wondrous modelling tool, capable of executing raised or sunken work at will, we require an instantaneous means of raising or reducing the air pressure. A convenient way of controlling the pressure, and, at the same time, carefully observing the work, is to connect a convenient length of very small india-rubber tube to the neck of the bulb, as shown by G, fig. 70. Let now the bulb G be the kind with the thick bottom shown at D. Holding the end, G', between the teeth (a small bushing of glass being inserted to facilitate this), the thick bottom of G is softened at the blowpipe flame, but obviously the bulb G cannot always be rotated in the same direction on account of the rubber tube, so the direction must be reversed from time to time. The bottom being softened, the bulb can be held upright fairly in front of the eyes and suction applied, whereby the hollowed bulb H is formed, a kind useful in certain thermometers and for other purposes. Obviously blowing would have given the form I, fig. 70. Here we have the basis of all that modelling and detailed work on bulbs with the blowpipe flame, which, in the hands of a skilled worker, may give wonderful representations of figures and animals in light-blown glass, like those formerly made in Venice, and lately revived to some extent. Somewhat similar articles are obtainable as "Cartesian divers," at shops where chemical apparatus is sold. In using the blowpipe flame as a modelling tool methods of working will almost suggest themselves, but I may point out how a tubular branch, sufficient for the limb of a figure, may be drawn from a bulb without joining on in the ordinary sense, and yet the branch may show as a different kind of glass. This kind of branching, which is common enough on some of the older hollow animals in glass, certainly puzzled me for years, but having found how it may be done, the thing becomes as obvious as all things do become when known. Let J, fig. 70, be a drawing-out from a larger tube ready for expansion into a bulb, and while hot, four patches of a similar glass (which, however, may be colored) are put on as shown; these patches being merely dabs made with a heated rod of glass, used much as a stick of sealing-wax is used. The piece being now heated several times and slightly expanded the patches will take the form of lens-like thickenings, this stage being suggested by K. The extent to which the patches spread over the bulb depends on the duration of the heatings, their number, and the degree of expansion. A rubber tube, as shown by G, fig. 70, is now adapted to K, and one of the lens-like thickenings is thoroughly heated through with a small flame, when a glass rod, K', only just softened at the extreme end, is brought centrally on the softened thickening. Now comes the most delicate part of the business: the main factor being a drawing by the rod, but this must be supplemented by a *very slight* internal air pressure, when the thickened part can be partly drawn and partly blown to the shape shown by L. The student who familiarises himself with other portions of the present book will now have little difficulty in realising how such a figure as M, fig. 70, may be made, the basis of the head being a second bulb on the stem above the main bulb. Before attempting any complex work in modelling on the bulb everything should be ready to hand for its completion; the piece should not be allowed to cool from beginning to finish. A sort of cosy of asbestos sheet and a careful fencing from occasional draughts are safeguards in such work. Complex articles with many branches also require careful annealing (see p. 169). The bottle shown by N, fig. 70, may be here sketched as an example of softened spots being made concave by internal suction.

Perforation of Soft Glass.—Perforation by a drill,

as already described, is completely inapplicable to light-blown work. A very usual way of blowing a hole is to close the tube or bulb to be perforated; let it be the tube A, fig. 71, and then to heat one spot with a small flame, as at A′. The enclosed air expanded by the heat now forces its way through the extremely soft glass, and a perforation results. More control over the nature of the perforation is

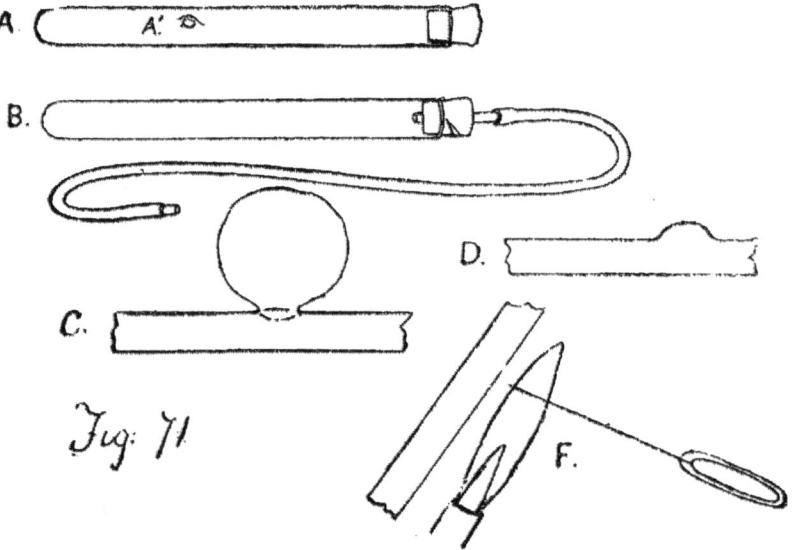

Fig. 71

obtained if a flexible blow-tube is used, as shown at B, fig. 71. If a small spot is intensely heated, and, while the heat is fully maintained, a gentle internal pressure of air is maintained, a hole as small as $\frac{1}{16}$ of an inch in diameter and having well-rounded edges can be made. By removing the glass from the flame and blowing sharply, the whole softened part blows out into a thin bursting bulb like C; and the thin glass being broken away, the edges can be rounded in the flame. In this way a perforation of almost any required size may be made. Sometimes it is convenient to first blow a little mound, as shown at D, and then to make the perforation at the apex. When several perforations are required on the same article by the blowing method it is obvious that those first made must be plugged or stopped to allow the work to continue. If the holes are large and far apart small cones or india-rubber plugs may be used; but if small or near together, conical plugs of asbestos may be used. A useful and convenient form of plug may be made from that asbestos paper which is now an article of commerce. Another method of perforating, which is specially convenient when a number of perforations are to be made close together, or when a hole is to be made for sealing in a platinum wire, is to draw out the required number of small tubular tails by the method described on p. 114, and illustrated by K and L, fig. 70; but for the drawing out of very small tubular tails it is neither necessary to thicken the glass as there described, nor to blow inside the piece during the drawing. The tails being cut off, holes remain, the sharp edges of which may be rounded off by heating. A third method, especially useful when very small holes are required in a very thin-walled tube or bulb, is to very intensely heat a platinum wire of about $\frac{1}{50}$ of an inch in diameter, and to push it through the glass. In order to do this successfully the glass must be held close to the side of the blowpipe flame as shown at F, fig. 71, the hot wire being pushed through the flame into the glass, and quickly withdrawn. The platinum wire is conveniently mounted in a glass handle, as shown; but an iron wire or even the tang of a file may be used. When iron is used a portion of the oxide of this metal generally attaches itself to the glass and often causes a fracture on cooling. A rather stout bulb, thoroughly softened by heat, may be perforated by a very quick stab with a point of the fine embroidery scissors already mentioned, this stab being a first step in the cutting open of the bulb. A slow movement of the scissors point against the softened bulb only indents it.

Bending Glass Tubes, Spirals.—Small tubes stout in the walls may be bent easily enough after being softened in the upper part of an ordinary fish-tail or bats-wing gas-burner. The tube should be held horizontally by the two hands (see fig. 72, A), rotated steadily, and the rotation should be accompanied by a slight but rapid lateral movement, to counteract any inequalities of the flame. The glass being now uniformly softened, bending is a very simple operation. This method is unsatisfactory, not only by reason of the deposit of soot which forms on the tube, but flint glass is often permanently blacked by reason of the reduction of the lead; and looking intently towards the luminous flame while the tube is being softened tends to prevent clear vision immediately afterwards. A much more satisfactory

SPIRALS. 119

arrangement is a bunsen or air burner giving a flat flame, but care must be taken that only the upper or "solid" part of the flame is used; and, in the case of small tubes, care must be taken not to over-heat the glass. A convenient form of bunsen or air burner is to be found in some of the asbestos gas-stoves sold for warming rooms. Such a burner,

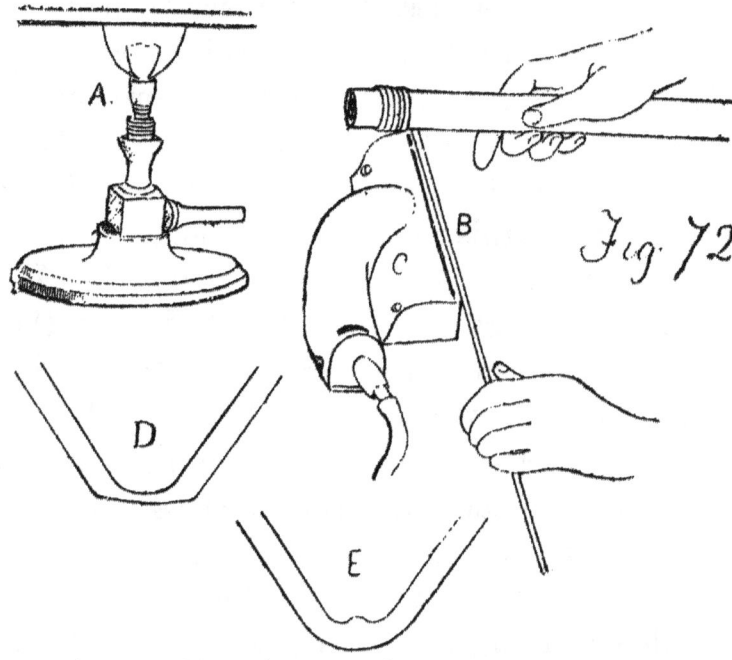

fig. 72, C, usually gives a flame 5 or 6 inches wide, but this width may be reduced by a sliding cap or inverted gutter made to fit over the top. In making a spiral from a small tube the full width of the flame is useful, the glass as softened being wound on a cylinder of wood covered with asbestos mill-board, the softened glass engaging on the cylinder from below, as shown by fig. 72, B. When cold, the wooden core is drawn out, and the asbestos can be removed. The mounting of the cylinder on bearings and the provision of a winch handle is a convenience, as a rate of turning can generally be found which just allows the tube to become softened in passing through the flame. Large tubes are best heated for softening, in the blowpipe flame, the gas being turned on so as to give a large but necessarily imperfect flame; but the lateral shift must be rapid, and of rather wide extent, so as to secure equal heating over a considerable length of the tube. In all cases of bending large tubes one end should be closed and the other end should be furnished with an india-rubber tube leading to the mouth, as shown by fig. 69, G. It will seldom be necessary to blow except during the act of bending, and then very gently. In bending a tube, that portion which forms the outside of the curve may be softer than that forming the inside. This may tend to such deformations as is shown by fig. 72, D, but it can be corrected afterwards by softening the flattened part and blowing out. The reverse deformation, fig. 72, E, results if the inside of the bend is hotter than the outside, and is not so easy to remedy.

Joining and Branching Tubes or Rods.—It is often impracticable to firmly and safely join together specimens of glass of widely differing composition or fusibility; hence, when several pieces have to be joined together, they should all, if possible, be made from glass of a similar character. As a rule, the presence of coloring matters in a glass base does not sufficiently alter its character or fusibility to affect the joining, although, when large quantities of iron and manganese are present, the glass becomes appreciably altered in the sense of being less viscous, and more distinctly fluid when heated.

Joining unlike Glasses.—When joining foreign glasses is unavoidable, the joint should be blown very thin, and, if possible, the joint should be in the substance of a bulb rather than in the course of a tube. A glass-blower may, in the present day of experimenting with vacuum tubes, be expected to securely join a length of the hardest combustion tube to a length of the softest flint glass, a by no means impossible performance if a series of steps are taken with rings of glasses of progressive fusibility by one of the methods indicated on p. 127, if all the joints are blown thin, and if the piece is thoroughly annealed. Annealing is desirable in all branched work, unless very small and thin-walled; but when joints between different kinds of glass are concerned, the utmost care should be taken not to allow the piece to cool before it is put into the annealing oven, and when here the heat should be lowered quite slowly. A specially difficult joint is often best annealed before the article is finished, if no more work is to be done close to the joint.

Plain Joining in one Straight Line.—Tubes to be joined, if not of nearly equal diameter, are best brought to about the same size at the part to be joined as by drawing out, as described in the text (p. 97), and illustrated by fig. 65. This drawing out may be either with or without thickening, as the case may require. An alternative method is to close the larger tube at the end (p. 101), and to blow a hole in the bottom (p. 115). Small tubes, say up to a diameter of 10 or 12 millimetres, are best if turned out a little, or opened at the mouth before being joined, as shown at fig. 73, A. One tube is closed at the end, the means of closing shown in the sketch being a short length of india-rubber tube and a plug of glass rod, the two forming a convenient cap; one end is left open for blowing. The tube A being held in one hand, and the tube B being held in the other, both are rotated so that the two expanded ends are heated at opposite parts of the flame, the object being to bring the extreme ends almost to a condition of liquid fusion, but for the heat to extend very little way up the stem. By the time the ends of the tubes are in a condition to be brought together, so much contraction may have taken place as to bring the form to that shown at C. If the softened ends are brought together while the glass is in the blowpipe flame, the turning should be continued, as the pause may result in so much unequal heating as to interfere with the next step; but, personally, I prefer to take the tubes from the flame for an instant, join and return to the flame for a few seconds—the turning being, of course, renewed. The open end is now applied to the mouth, as shown at D, when a slight, drawing motion, with a very little increase of pressure inside, will

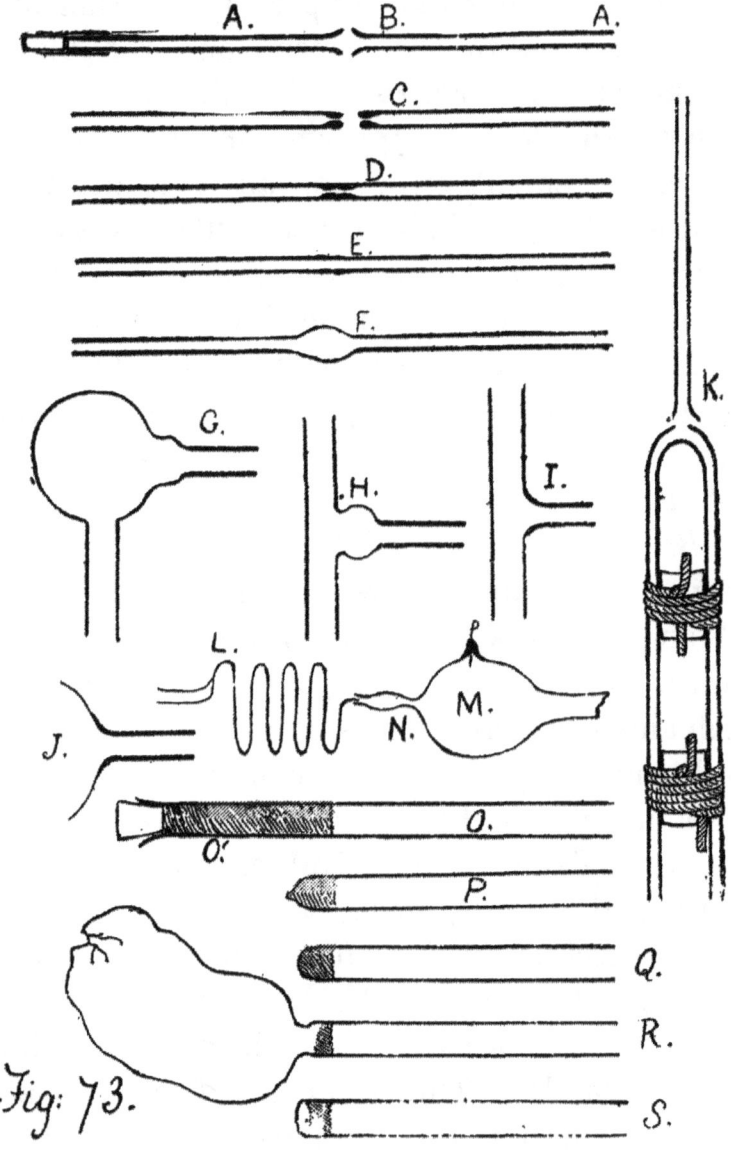

Fig. 73.

bring the joint to the shape shown at E. If the glasses are dissimilar in character, it is, as already suggested, safer to blow the joint out more, as at F. When the tube A is very long, the far end of it should rest in a fork-like support, the worker should be fairly end on to the system, and the blowpipe flame should shoot across. If both tubes are very long, both should be supported in the above way, and it is convenient either for an assistant to blow or to use a flexible india-rubber tube, as shown by fig. 70, G, and with the precaution as to the occasional reversal of the turning, which is mentioned on p. 113. The sketch will sufficiently illustrate the position of things in joining small to large end on, but in this diagram the essential of one closed end is not indicated.

A Branch on a Large Tube or on a Bulb.—A hole corresponding approximately with the diameter of the branch is blown, as described on p. 116, and all openings but this hole being closed, the end of the branch and the surroundings of the hole are intensely heated, and brought together as described in the last paragraph for straight tubes, but the return of the piece to the flame for a revival of the heat is often difficult at this stage, owing to a possibly awkward shape; therefore it is often convenient to blow cautiously at this stage. Under these circumstances one obtains a joint such as is shown in section in fig. 73, G or H. This form, in which the actual joint is blown out very thin, is admirable from a laboratory point of view, as not being liable to break under sudden changes of temperature, but it looks unneat, and would be scarcely tolerated in the case of a commercial article. By getting the contacting parts of the glass intensely hot, and joining at the right instant, avoiding any draw, and giving the very slightest expansion by the breath, joints like I and J can be made in the first instance, but if a more uniform distribution of the glass is required, it is seldom practicable to obtain it by heating the whole joint to the full softening heat. One has rather to go round the joint area by area, heating a small proportion to the utmost softness, and very slightly blowing each spot out. Then all the course round the joint must be brought to a moderate degree of viscosity, when it is rounded off by gentle blowing. For the above small area or spot by spot work, it is a great convenience to use the flexible rubber blowing tube, as shown by fig. 69, G, and described on p. 113.

A Branch on a Small Tube.—The manipulation is precisely as described above, only the small tube must be fastened down to a support with gap in it, such as that shown by fig. 51 and described on p. 59. A handle, as shown by the dotted area A, fig. 51, is a considerable convenience when the tube on which the branch is joined is short, as it makes it easy to turn the piece for heating all round the joint. When a branch is to be joined on at the end of a loop made in another tube, as in certain forms of sprengel pump, the two limbs are tied together by binding knots with blocks of cork between, as shown by fig. 73, K, and then the operation is much the same as in joining two tubes end to end.

Joining Rods, or Rods to Tubes.—Two rods, each melted to a globule at the end, as shown by fig. 62, E, and described on p. 92, will unite perfectly if gently placed together, and if the joint be very slightly pulled out as it cools. The joining of a rod to a tube is a precisely similar operation. The branching of rods is most conveniently done by clamping all on a light wooden frame and heating the point of union until it spheroids; adding more glass if required. Such joints require careful annealing.

Joining Capillary Tubes, and connecting Vacuum Vessels to Pump.—A rigid connection between the mercurial pump and any vessel to be exhausted is very undesirable as conducive to fracture, especially at the narrow neck ordinarily left close to the vessel for sealing off. A capillary tube, varying, say, from 1 to $1\frac{1}{2}$ millimetres in its external diameter, is drawn from the inlet of the pump, and this may be conveniently bent backwards or forwards, as shown by fig. 73, L, to give a convenient flexibility. The most generally useful exhaustion branch for a vacuum vessel is one drawn out like fig. 70, L, but not expanded quite so much by blowing, and afterwards drawn down fine near to the vessel, as shown at M, fig. 73, where the small end of the drawing out is shown as close to the end of the capillary tube L joined to the pump. Things being in this position, a good join can be made by bringing a bunsen burner flame downwards, where one tube enters into the other. Such a connection is much to be preferred to an india-rubber connection covered by mercury or glycerine, and takes far less time to make. A fresh length of capillary tube can always be joined to L as required.

Joining together very Short Lengths of Tube, forming a Stem of Ring-like Pieces.—This operation may often arise in decorative work with glasses of different color, also in making the successive steps of a stable connection between a highly refractory glass and an easily fusible glass (see p. 64). Let O, fig. 73, be a tube to which O' has been joined. O' is now drawn off, as shown at P, the seal is rounded, as shown at Q, after which the bottom is heated and blown out to the thin bursting bulb shown by R. The thin glass being broken away and the end heated we have S, which is the original tube O to which a short length of O' is attached; the end being open and ready for the same operation to be repeated with another tube. In performing this operation glass in the form of rod or scrap will often have to be used, as in making the stable connection between extremes of fusibility it is quite unreasonable to suppose that the glass-blower would have all gradations as tube—indeed, in most cases he would have to prepare the intermediate glasses himself by crushing the two originals and mixing the powders in various proportions. In this case the mixture would be gathered into a lump on a ring of platinum wire; this being heated and repeatedly dipped into the mixture of powders. Such a gathering, or a mass, from the end of a softened rod, would be attached to the tube O, blown to a small thick bulb, rolled on a tile to reduce the bulge to the diameter of the tube, after which the bottom would be blown out, as shown at R; when brought to the condition S all would be ready for the next step. Obviously, in the case supposed, O should be the least fusible of the two glasses.

Air Traps and various Internal Sealings.—The most common kind of internal sealing is an air trap, like that on a barometer column, shown at fig. 74, A. It is most conveniently made as follows. B is a portion of the barometer tubing, to which has been joined a piece of larger diameter and thinner in the side (see p. 122). The projecting portion of the air trap (see p. 97) being placed inside, the open end is sealed (see p. 101 and 103), giving the form C. Being held as at D and rotated, the end is heated and slightly blown out as at D, a very little adjustment to gravity bringing the point to a central position, when the bottom is expanded. A small flame is now used to soften so much of the bottom as lies within the central tube, when this is blown to a thin bursting bulb, E, and broken away with the fingers or a file. A final join is made to the rest of the barometer tube, as indicated by F (see p. 122). A good illustration of another style of internal sealing is afforded by the vacuum jacketed flask, which may be used to prevent the

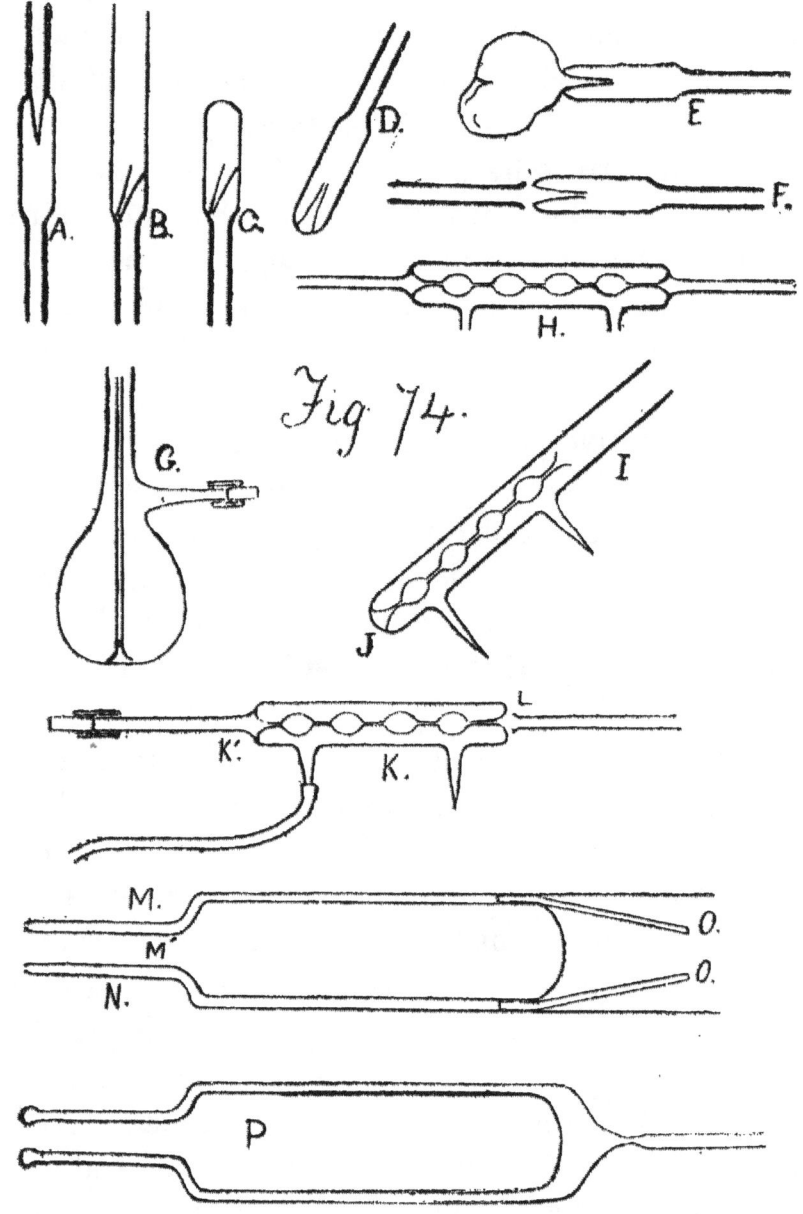

Fig. 74.

access of heat to such highly volatile fluids as liquid

air. A flask, **M'**, is made by methods already indicated, and the mouth of this is turned out a little so as to about meet the turning in of the outer jacket, **N**. Strips of cork are now placed as indicated by O O, to keep the inside flask steadily in position, when the mouth is heated in the blowpipe flame, so that the two tubes forming the double mouth run together; the first joining being assisted, if necessary, by a little local pressure with a rod of gas carbon, or the male and female cones, fig. 48, A and B, may be used to expand and contract the inside and outside respectively. When the union is complete a slight air-pressure applied at the large open end will expand the mouth to the shape shown in the next figure, P. The pieces of cork being now removed, the large tube is drawn down as shown, a small tail being left for connecting with the mercurial pump, as shown by fig. 73, L M. A double internal sealing like H, fig. 74, involves no real departure from the way of making the first described air trap. I J represents the main outer tube with the internal portion laid in position, and the sealed end, J, is heated until complete union has taken place, when a gentle pressure of air serves to round off the end, after which the central portion is perforated, as in the case of the air trap first described, and one end piece is joined on as indicated at K'. One of the side branches is now opened, and it is convenient to attach a piece of small rubber tube as shown. The outer tube is next drawn over the internal piece and heated, until union takes place, when the end is rounded off by slight air-pressure through the side opening; the centre is perforated as before, and the other end tube is joined. Finally, the side branches are cut off and turned out, when we have a convenient form of Liebig's condenser; but a somewhat similar construction is more common as a jacketed vacuum tube. An inner seal, which is used merely as a support for a tube, is shown by G, fig. 74, a fine tube having a perforation in the lower part of its side standing in the small flask as shown. The central tube, in which the perforation has previously been made, and slightly funnel-shaped at the lower end, is placed loosely in the flask, and the bottom is heated until union takes place, when the join is rounded off by a slight air-pressure. The article is a spray-producer, but the neck is ordinarily bent to nearly a right-angle, no special precautions being required in bending, as with moderate heating the two tubes have no tendency to adhere. The main points to attend to in air-trap work and internal sealing are to avoid thick masses of glass, to see that all is well rounded off, to guard against lateral adhesions of contiguous surfaces, and not to allow the piece to cool before it is put into the annealing oven. A thorough annealing is always desirable in the case of work with internal sealings.

Making Rods and Tubes at the Blowpipe.—Considering that $1\frac{1}{2}$ ounces of glass is rather a large quantity to thoroughly soften at a blowpipe worked by a foot power bellows, it is obvious that long and heavy rods and tubes are not to be made at the blowpipe table, but it is often a great convenience to make short lengths of small diameter from scraps of broken glass; indeed, to the blowpipe worker no scrap of broken colored glass is without interest. The making of ordinary glass tubes and rods in the glass-house is as follows, and this method slightly modified is available for blowpipe work. What the worker in the glass-house calls a blowpipe is a

Fig. 75.

straight iron tube, and by repeatedly dipping this in the pot of molten glass and allowing a short time for each quantity to cool a little, a mass of viscous glass of almost any required size can be gathered at the end of the blowpipe. To make a tube, such a mass is blown hollow, rolled to an approximately cylindrical form on an iron slab called a marver (from French, *marbre*), or stretched to a cylindrical shape by swinging. An iron rod called a punty (from French, *pointille*), on the end of which is a mass of soft glass, is now attached to the elongated

MAKING RODS AND TUBES. 133

bulb, as indicated by fig. 75. The two workmen now walk apart, turning their two rods in unison, and the tube is drawn out to the required length. The same considerations as those put forward on p. 97 determine the degree of parallelism of the tube, and it is a common thing for boys to run to and fro fanning the thinner parts to chill them. The rotation is kept up till the tube is fairly rigid, when it is laid down on a kind of ladder, as shown by fig. 76. The long cane is finally cut into lengths and annealed. Rods are made in the same way, only the

Fig. 76.

original mass is not blown hollow. The blowpipe operation is very similar. A ball or mass (see fig. 62 on p. 79) is gathered on the end of a length of hard Bohemian tube (the combustion tubing of the chemical laboratory), and this mass, whether blown hollow or otherwise, is drawn out, a piece of glass rod, the end of which is softened by heat, serving as a handle. In this case the drawing out of a hollow mass may range from the production of what may be regarded as an elongated bulb to a long fine tube. Fig. 68, A, A', C, D, E, and the description p. 107, indicate methods by which elongated bulbs or tubes of almost any proportion may be made at the blowpipe from glass originally procured as rod; but the gathering or globule shown at B and B', fig. 68, may be formed of scrap or other glass melted to a ball on the end of a tobacco pipe stem, or on a rod or "punty" of less fusible glass. Instead of drawing the bulb into a tube by attaching a "punty" and pulling, it is often very much better to take advantage of gravity in some such way as the following, especially when a short tube with thick walls is wanted :—Let A, fig. 77, be the bulb of

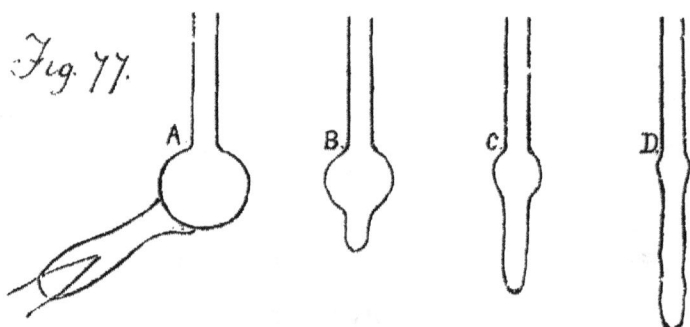

scrap glass which has been formed on the end of a tube of less fusible glass. This bulb being held with the shaft vertical in front of a blowpipe flame can be elongated, as shown by B, C, and D. When one has any special glass in the form of thin rod, or as a sheet which can be cut into narrow strips by means of a glazier's diamond, and a short piece of tube is wanted, the rods or strips can be grouped and bound round two asbestos cylinders, one of which is perforated. It is then drawn, and blown as required, excepting so far as the latter operation is dependent on the closeness with which the strips are laid together. This method of making a short piece of tube from strips or rods is more especially of interest in connection with striped or threaded tubes.

Twisted, Striped, Composite, and other Tubes or Rods.—The possibilities in the above directions are very wide, and the neck of a small ornamental bottle will often be treated independently of the bulb. This branch of work has most interest in connection with the making of such small decorative articles as are treated of in Chapter IX. And in connection with this subject short notes will serve as affording sufficient suggestions to persons following up this line of work.

Twisted Rods.—Several soft masses of glass laid together and twisted while being drawn out will give a great variety of effect. If the twisting is continued after the glass begins to chill, the rod will often be in such tension as to break up spontaneously. Heating to the softening point and slow cooling in the annealing chamber give a remedy.

Spiral of Air in a Stem or Rod.—This effect, very common in the older Venetian work, is quite easy to obtain;—a small air-bubble between two masses, which are drawn out and twisted while very hot, giving a well-shaped spiral in a smooth stem. Several ways of introducing the air-bubble will suggest themselves according to the conditions of work, but in case of two soft masses, each at the end of a rod, A and B, fig. 78, the easiest way is to quickly stab one with such a pointed tool as C, and before the wound has closed A and B are placed together, fully heated, then drawn and twisted, these stages being shown by D and E.

Striped Tubes.—One method with strips or rods is sufficiently indicated at the end of a previous section (p. 135). Another is to lay patches of foreign glass on a bulb, or a mass which is to become a bulb, much in the same way as shown by I and K, fig. 70, and described on p. 114, and to

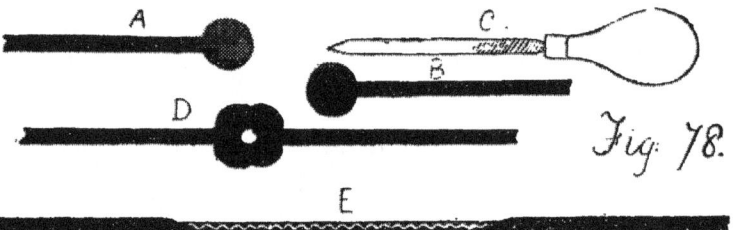

blow and draw as may be required. Other methods will suggest themselves in working.

Spiraled Tubes.—If a striped tube is twisted in drawing out it becomes spiraled.

Cased or Flashed Tubes or Bulbs.—The rudimentary bulb, or the mass from which it is to be blown, may be rolled in the colored glass crushed (see p. 137) to a fine powder, or a glass-painter's color may be used in the same way, but several blowings out and re-heatings may be required to make the outer layer smooth. In a somewhat similar way a powdered glass may be made to line the inside of a bulb by shaking and turning. Fig. 68, I, and the description on p. 110, will sufficiently indicate another way of flashing or plating the outside of a bulb or the tube drawn from it, the outer sleeve shown being of the required colored glass.

Crushing or powdering Glass. — This is often necessary. The best instrument for small quantities is the steel mortar, fig. 79. A lump of glass being placed as shown, the pestle is struck by a mallet. The fine powder is sifted out, and the coarse can be returned to be again crushed. Glass enamels and

vitrified materials generally can be crushed to rather fine powder in the steel mortar. When still finer grinding is required an agate mortar shown by fig. 80 should be used.

Threads—Spun Glass.—If a mass of soft glass is touched with a piece of solid glass and this latter is quickly withdrawn, the soft glass is pulled out to a very fine thread, and if this thread is connected to the circumference of a wheel, the whole of the soft mass may be wound off as a fine thread, provided that the heat of the mass is maintained. For thus making a considerable hank of spun glass it is necessary to have a grooved wheel rapidly revolving in a plane which cuts the hot part of the flame. The starting end of the thread is drawn out and given one rapid turn round the revolving wheel. Sometimes a gap is left in the circumference of the wheel, so that the mass of threads can be cut off; but if a closed hank is wished for, one flange of the wheel must be removable. I have found it convenient to use a wheel actuated by a small fan motor worked by a blast from the bellows. The spun glass when mounted in a handle makes a brush which can be used for strong acids.

Feet, Claws, and Syringe Handle Flats.—The flattening of the bottom of a bulb to make a standing flask has been already described (pp. 113 and 102). The simplest form of separate foot is very easy to make, and the stages are shown by fig. 81. A is an article (a test tube) to which a foot is to be added, and the end being drawn off and sealed as shown, a similarly drawn off piece of tube is joined on as indicated. For cutting off this piece at the point indicated by the arrow, the cold (and maybe damped) file method on the hot glass (see p. 80) is best, and should not the fissure go evenly round the tube, the end must be trimmed by the scissors (see p. 84). To spread out the foot as shown at B, the edges are softened in the flame, and while the piece is being revolved on its axis, the foot is spread out with one of the carbon turnpins held as shown. The main point in success is not to heat the foot so far in as to soften the narrow stem, otherwise the foot will bend over and

FEET, CLAWS, FLATS.

the work will be spoiled. To make the article stand quite upright, the edges of the foot are softened, and the article is brought down vertically on a slab as shown at C. A final heating to a temperature just short of the softening point is desirable in this case, as in all other cases where glass may have been

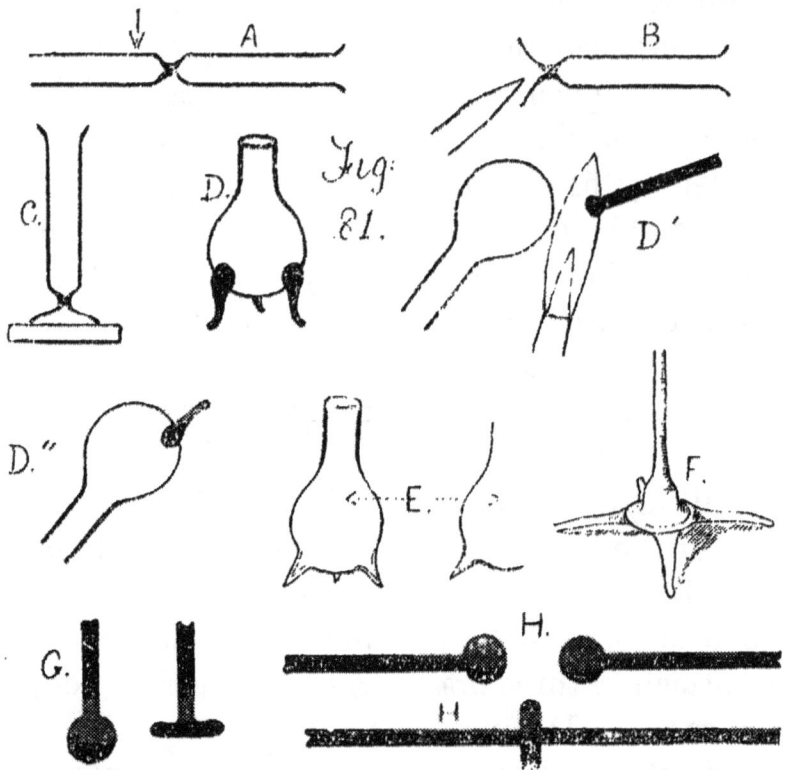

Fig. 81.

suddenly chilled. The little flask, D, fig. 81, illustrates a very ready way of making solid branches which serve as feet. A small ball of molten glass is gathered on the end of a scrap of rod or tube, and the part of the bulb is held opposite, just so near the flame as to be short of softening, the right point being for most glasses just where the object begins to tint the flame. The hot glass being now brought in contact with the bulb, is drawn out while in the flame, when it will melt off to a blunt end as shown at D″. Very perfect union between the bulb and the foot can be obtained by this method if the temperature of the bulb is right; but, owing to the sudden difference of thickness, subsequent breakage is likely to happen, unless careful annealing follows. Three legs, as shown at E, fig. 81, by the method illustrated by fig. 70, L, and described on p. 114, are far more stable, and for small articles no annealing is required. After a great many experiments on a stable and satisfactory claw-pillar for small articles, I arrived at the form shown by F, fig. 81, a form which is easy to make, and has no heavy massing of the glass likely to cause spontaneous fracture, even if a small article is unannealed. To the drawn out bottom of the vase is first attached a bell, like the foot of B (fig. 81) in its first stage. The edge of this bell is somewhat thickened in the flame, and to it are attached three branches by the method adopted in the case of D, and shown by D′ and D″. As these are attached to the somewhat thickened edge of the bell (F, fig. 81), there is not that massing close to a very thin part which tends so much to fracture. In any case, the adjustment of the length and angle of each foot, so that the object stands upright, is a very easy matter; a little being drawn off as required, or any foot being bent as found necessary after a trial standing on a level slab. The well-known flats on the handle of an ordinary glass syringe are very simply made. The flat at the end is simply a globule melted on the rod (see fig. 62, and description p. 92), and flattened by pressure on the asbestos-covered table or on a tile (see G, fig. 81). The flats in the course of the rod are made by compressing two globules together as shown at H, and H′, fig. 81.

Handles, Rings, Eyes.—Loop handles and eyes for hanging are attached to many small articles,—the weights of the wheel barometer, for instance, and some kinds of thermometer; also suspension plummets for determining the gravity of a liquid by the loss of weight of a solid suspended in it. All typical cases are illustrated by sketches on pp. 139 and 142. Fig. 82, A, shows a small flask with loop suspension. The flask, B, being held inverted, let us say, by the tongs, fig. 49, I, the concave extremities of which are served with asbestos thread, the two parts composing the loop are put on, as shown by fig. 81, D′ and D″, and explained on p. 139, stability being secured (see p. 140) by joining the elements of the loop on the slightly thickened margin. The drawing of the two ends, and fusing the join into a little globule, scarcely needs remark. C shows a similar operation on a rod which may be intended for a barometer weight or a specific-gravity plummet. Assuming the superfluous glass to be drawn off at the narrow place, as suggested by C, fig. 82, it becomes an easy matter to round off the eye to the shape shown by C'. For this purpose the end is generally softened; and as the eye rapidly contracts, this tendency is balanced by quick prods from alternate sides with a pointed turnpin of carbon (see p. 58) like C''. A touch or two on the side pro-

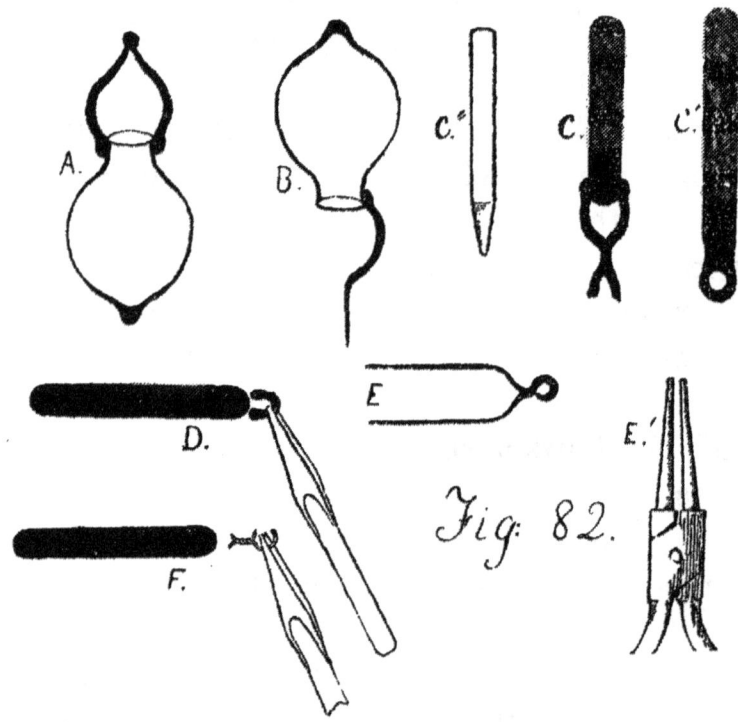

jections with the same tool may be necessary, but all the rest may be left to the natural surface-tension of the softened glass. Putting a staplelike piece on the softened end, as at D, fig. 82, looks simpler on paper, but is not quicker in execution than the method just described, and generally gives a weaker eye. The eyelet shown at E, fig. 82, and usual on encased thermometers, is easily made by rapidly bending a projecting tail with small round-nosed pliers, E', and reheating so as to unite the glass at the turn of the eye. It is often much better to make a suspension eye of thin platinum wire than of glass, the twisted shank being embedded in the end of a softened rod, as shown at F, fig. 82, or the wire may be sealed in a hollow end, as described under the heading " Electrodes " (p. 150).

Grinding Pistons to Cylinders — Grinding Stoppers and Stopcock Plugs.—Such cylinder and piston work as one finds in the usual glass syringe, the piston of which is packed with cotton, requires no remark, the two special points in making the ordinary syringe being treated of on pp. 141 and 99. For laboratory work, syringes without cotton packing are required; and a pattern which I have found it quite easy to construct, and which is suitable for work with acids, corrosive fluid, and in bacteriological research, is shown by fig. 83. Assuming tha one has tubing of the necessary sizes and exactness, the construction of the syringe will offer no difficulty to one who has mastered the operations already described. The bulb, B, should pass through the drawn-in portion, A; and the drawing out of the point, C, D or E, is done after the piston is placed in position. In a large selection of glass tubing some pieces may often be selected by which such a syringe as the above may be constructed, which shall be sufficiently tight for drawing off acids and other such uses, without any grinding of the working surfaces. In this case the tightness depends upon an annulus of the liquid being held by capillarity between the piston and the cylinder, and as long as this annulus is intact the tightness is absolute. This tightness is only good against low pressure, but almost any required degree of tightness may be realised if the piston and cylinder are fitted by

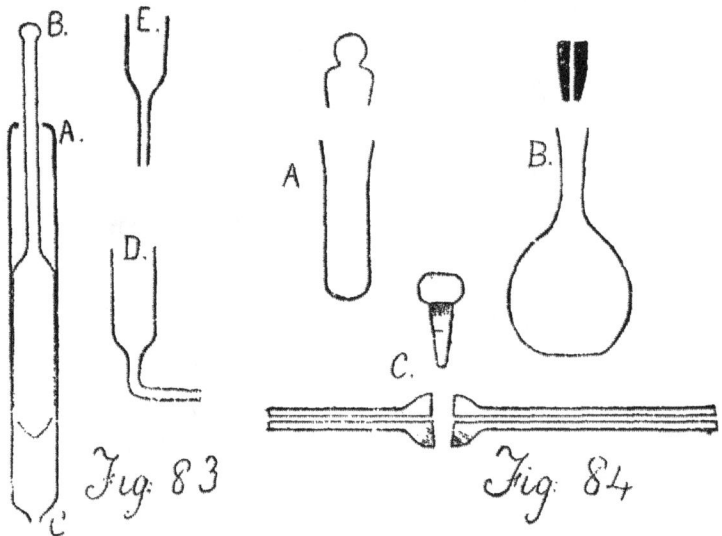

grinding. The unground glass syringe, to be used only for decanting under low pressure, will naturally have a larger aperture at the mouth, as shewn at C; but when a good fit between piston and cylinder is obtained by grinding, as described below, it becomes practicable to have such points as D or E, and to eject under some pressure. Pieces of tube should be carefully selected for roundness, parallelism, and freedom from internal projections, and they should

GRINDING CYLINDERS AND PISTONS.

be no thicker in the wall than is essential. Flint glass is generally best for this work. The tube selected for the piston should just fail to enter the outer tube. No grinding tools I have made for this class of work have proved so satisfactory as the commercial mandril-drawn brass tubing, which may be considered to be obtainable of every size between half an inch and an inch in diameter, as the very slight tapering of the long lengths more than covers any difference between the running sizes. This tubing is obtainable at Smith's metal warehouse, St John's Square, Clerkenwell. A length of the mandril-drawn tube, which will easily enter the glass tube to be ground internally, and twice as long as the glass tube, having been selected, is mounted on the lathe with the glass tube over it, the interspace being well supplied with the finest flour emery and paraffin oil. The lathe being set in motion, the glass tube is worked to and fro with the hand, also back against the motion of the central tube, until the whole surface or nearly the whole surface is ground,—the glass being occasionally reversed on the brass tube. The piston, like that shown by fig. 83, is best made before it is ground; and for grinding, a trough cut from mandril-drawn brass tube, of suitable size is used, this trough being supplied with the mixture of paraffin oil and fine flour emery. I have found that working the piston backwards and forwards in the trough is more convenient than using the lathe in this case.

Grinding Stoppers.—In almost all cases when the glass-blower wishes to stopper any vessel, the mouth is swelled out by a turnpin (see p. 93), and the piece to form the stopper is drawn to something like a corresponding slope. Thus in fig. 84, A represents a tube and hollow stopper made as they would be before the actual operation of stoppering is commenced, while B shows a specific-gravity bottle and its hollow stopper of thermometer tubing in a similar condition. After what has been said about the general methods of working, no special instructions are needed for making these articles. The stopper and its seating may be separately ground, with metal cones of suitable angle, similar to those shown by fig. 53, F and G, and they are afterwards ground together with a mixture of emery and paraffin oil (see p. 85).

Stopcocks.—These are most frequently made in a considerable thickening on a piece of tube, fig. 84, C, the hole for the plug being first cut out by one of the methods already described (pp. 86 and 87), and then ground out conical with the stoppering tool just mentioned. The cross head of the plug can be made by melting up a spheroid and flattening it, and the grinding of the plug in position is merely an operation of stoppering, as already described. The small hole across the plug must be drilled (see p. 86).

The Opening of a broad-rimmed Mouth on a Bulb; the Thistle Funnel. — The opening up of broad-

THE THISTLE FUNNEL.

rimmed mouths, either on a bulb or on the end of a tube, is a frequently occurring operation, and is perhaps best illustrated by the process of making a thistle-headed funnel, the stages of which are shown by fig. 85. (1) To the small tube, A, forming the shaft of the funnel, is joined (see p. 120) a piece of thick-walled and larger tube, B. (2) This larger tube is drawn off (p. 101) and rounded (p. 103) as shown at C; then (3) blown into a thick-bottomed

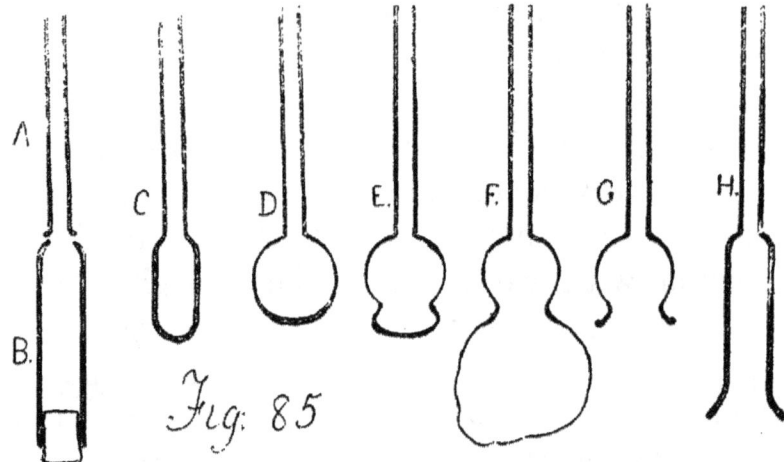

Fig. 85

bulb, D. (4) The thick part is now heated, and an expansion, E, is blown on the bulb. (5) The bottom of this expansion is next strongly heated, with as sharp a line of demarcation between the heated bottom and the sloping margin as possible, and energetic blowing expands the heated part to a thin bursting bulb, as shown at F. (6) The thin glass being broken away, the extreme margin of the bevelled part is melted, the flame now completing the funnel, G. As a rule, any attempt to turn out or otherwise manipulate the mouth of a thistle funnel spoils it. If the head of the thistle funnel is gripped by such a holding tool as fig. 49, C, the shaft may be drawn off close to the bottom, and the soft bottom may be flattened on a tile, forming a kind of basin, or a little spiral shaft and foot (pp. 140 and 135) may be added to form a small vase. The same kind of broad-rimmed mouth may be blown on the original large tube, forming a long cylindrical funnel, H; indeed, this way of opening the closed end of a tube is often more convenient than cutting off the end.

Moulding and Pressing.—Blowing into a mould, although a very common operation when bottles are made at a glass-house, is not much practised in connection with work before the blowpipe, except in the case of some of the Thuringian glass toys; but every glass-blower may now and then employ the method with advantage, especially when a number of small bulbs of irregular pattern are required. A mould for blowpipe work very nearly resembles a bullet mould; and if a little ball of hot glass, A, fig. 86, at the end of a small tube, be introduced into the cavity of a bullet mould, it can be blown out against the inside of the mould. Wood or cork may be used in making the mould, these materials soon becoming carbonised inside; but generally it is better to make the casings of the mould as thin iron boxes, and to fill them in with a material which can be packed round a pattern, plaster of paris

MOULDING AND PRESSING. 149

being very suitable in this respect. It should be well dried, and blackleaded inside. Perhaps the very best material for a mould is fine blacklead compressed tightly round a metal pattern, but the sharp edges are easily damaged. It need scarcely be said that moulds of plaster or blacklead must be hot when used. The term "moulding" is generally applied to the operation of blowing a hollow article in a mould; and the term "pressing" to the shaping of

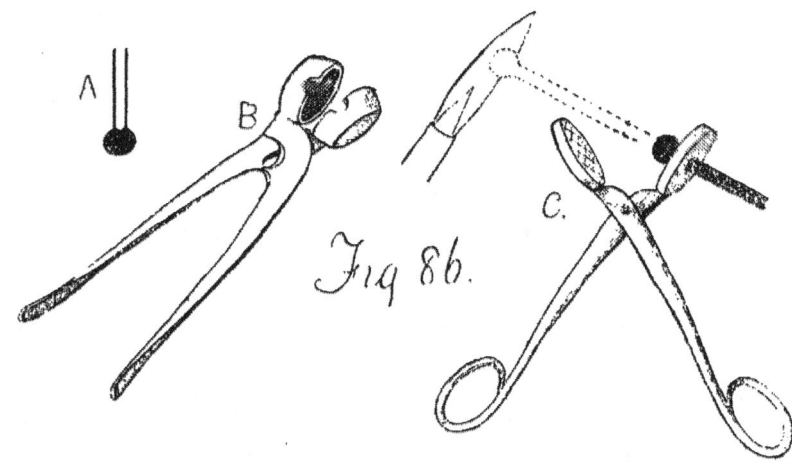

Fig 86.

glass by pinching the soft glass between rigid surfaces, and by this latter process many small articles are made with surprising perfection, especially in Paris and Venice. Artificial gems, with facets almost as bright as if they were cut and polished, are made by pinching a little ball of colored glass between dies mounted pincer fashion; and seals pressed by the same process might in some cases almost pass for antique engraved gems; while pressed medallions, doubtless made in a similar way, were used in ancient times, but whether as coins or weights has been a matter of dispute. Stamps or types of glass appear to have been made and used in Venice by Panfilo Castaldi for the printing of initial and ornamental letters, a little before the time ordinarily looked upon as that of the introduction of printing; and he is said subsequently to have printed whole broadsides of movable wooden types (see Wallace-Dunlop, *Glass in the Old World*, p. 145). Indeed, Faust is said to have visited Castaldi; and some of Castaldi's broadsides are said to be still in existence. For certain purposes pressed glass types may be useful in the present day, and the idea has recently been revived. Perhaps the best method of making a seal, stamp, or type at the end of a rod is that suggested by fig. 86.

Electrodes.—In practice, platinum is the only metal which can be sealed into the walls of a glass vessel to carry an electric current or discharge, and the satisfactory sealing in of platinum electrodes is a matter of considerable practical importance. Fig. 87, A, represents the method which I am inclined to regard as the best and most stable method of sealing a wire into the end of a tube,—that is to say, the best as regards complete tightness and non-liability to spontaneous fracture, although on most commercial articles the inside seal, as shown at D″, is generally expected. To make the seal, A, the tube is drawn out to a rather thick end (see p. 98), and the platinum wire, temporarily attached

SEALING IN ELECTRODES.

to a waste piece of glass as a handle, is inserted, and the glass of the long stem is thoroughly fused round it. Before the seal cools, the glass handle is crushed off the wire, and the wire is looped as at A, the free end being embedded so as to close the

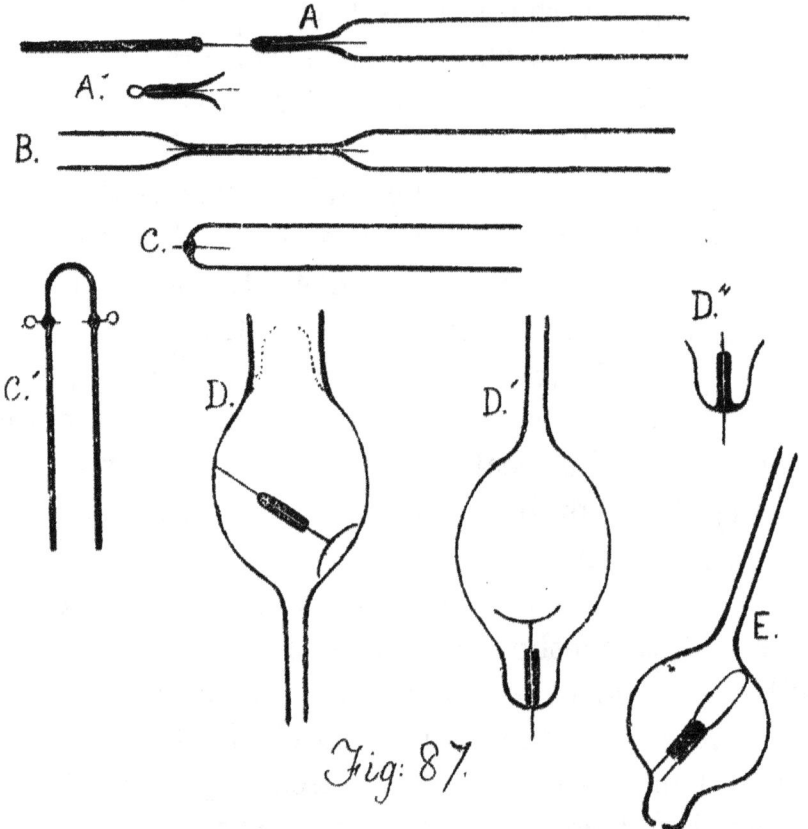

Fig. 87.

loop. A modification of this seal, by which it can be made on the exhaustion branch of a vacuum tube, —an advantage in the case of very small tubes, and I have made vacuum tubes as small as $\frac{1}{8}$ of an inch long inside,—is described by me in the *Amateur Photographer* for May 1, 1896 (p. 382). The mode of making this kind of seal is indicated at B, fig. 87, the platinum wire being placed in the tube leading to the vacuum pump; this part being drawn out until the bore is only a little over the diameter of the platinum wire. The exhaustion being complete, the narrow tube round the wire is heated, so that the glass becomes compressed around the wire. When the tube is cold, the extreme portion on the wire can be crushed by nippers without interfering with the seal. The end of the seal can be rounded off by melting, and the free end of the wire turned back into the soft glass to make a loop. The style of sealing as shown at C and C′ is not generally satisfactory, and is now seldom employed except in the case of the spark wires of a eudiometer. For this seal, perforation by drawing out a tail (p. 117), or by the hot platinum wire (p. 118), is generally most suitable. The platinum wire should be attached to a temporary glass handle, as in the first method, and a small bead should be melted on the wire where the seal is to be made. Hole and bead being now intensely heated, the wire is placed in position, and, if necessary, a slight expansion is effected by blowing. The internal seal, with a long coating of glass on the wire inside the tube, is most in favour for commercial work, and this despite the fact that in many—perhaps most—cases the long inner protection of the wire is inoperative, by reason of a fissure just inside the seal. Any internal garniture is fused on to the platinum wire,

SEALING IN ELECTRODES.

and the outer end is attached to a temporary glass handle. A thread is now wrapped round to form the internal clothing, this being easier to do just at the top of a bunsen burner than in the blowpipe flame, the winding on of the thread being performed so that the thread comes on from underneath (see fig. 72, B). Overheating at this stage must be avoided, or the glass will flow away from the wire, which will then become uncentral; but taking advantage of the glass handle as facilitating rotation, there will be no difficulty in thoroughly fusing the glass on the wire. The glass handle being now crushed off, the electrode is placed inside its tube or bulb, as shown at D (fig. 87), and the neck is brought down to its final shape, rounded off, and perforated, as shown by the dotted lines. The electrode being now brought into the position shown by D', is sealed in just the same way as the air-trap tube (p. 128), or the central tube of the spray producer; and in gently blowing out, the form D" should be aimed at. One of the quickest and best methods of sealing the wires and filament into an incandescent lamp involves a procedure so similar to that last described that the sketch E, fig. 87, scarcely requires explanation. The filament attached to a platinum loop, the arms of which loop pass through a small flat block of glass, is placed in the bulb by the large neck; and this neck being contracted generally by a pair of pincers so as to leave a flat opening, the mounted filament is shaken into position and sealed in, the external wire being then cut and turned back so as to form the two eyelets. One of the best glasses for electrode work is a special soft german glass, similar to the ordinary soft soda glass, but containing about 15 per cent. of oxide of lead,—this glass being now largely manufactured for making incandescent lamps. With suitable precautions (see p. 121), it can be joined satisfactorily to either ordinary flint glass or soft soda glass.

Connecting Glass Tubes to Metal Fittings.—Many methods of doing this are so well known as to need no remark or description; but when high pressures

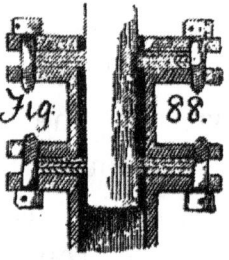

are concerned, the method indicated by fig. 88 is perhaps the very best. The washers may range from soft rubber to lead, according to pressure and circumstances: obviously, in the latter case the metal fittings and screws would have to be heavier and stronger than the sketch suggests, as the lead would have to be squeezed out laterally against the glass tube.

Graduated Scales on Glass.—To fully deal with all the problems of graduation which may occasionally arise in connection with the work of the glass-blower would involve a treatise in itself. I therefore propose to confine myself mainly to a short general account of the more common operations, and a description of some modified methods which I have found to be specially valuable in everyday work. *Common Glass Measures for Fluids.*—Conical graduated glasses used by pharmaceutical chemists are graduated by weighing or measuring quantities of water corresponding to each step into the glass, and the lines, figures, and signs are engraved with a minute copper wheel rotating at high speed, and charged with diamond dust or fine emery together with oil; but in the case of such measures, conventionality of appearance is considered of far more importance than accuracy, as medicinal dosing is seldom so finely adjusted a matter as to be seriously affected by a variation of even 10 per cent. *The more accurate Measures for Fluids.*—In the case of the more accurate measures intended for technical uses and the rougher laboratory purposes, the aim is generally to make the measure as accurately cylindrical as practicable; then a few points are determined by experiment, and each section is divided on the outside of the cylinder into divisions of equal length. This kind of method, if supplemented by making special determinations for the bottom divisions, and by making the successive degrees on each section graduatedly unequal (as described below) when the measure tapers, is capable of a very high degree of accuracy, and will serve all ordinary needs.

If, on the other hand, the utmost possible accuracy is required on a graduated glass instrument, an arbitrary scale is ordinarily engraved upon it, and the value of each degree is determined, entry being made in a calibration book. When a scale—let us say, a scale of millimetres—has to be simply copied upon a glass tube, on a strip of glass, or even on a strip of paper, the operation is very easy, and is ordinarily performed as follows:—

Copying a Scale.—Let A A, fig. 89, be the original scale, fixed down to a table opposite the left hand of the operator by means of a rigid metal strip, B B, the front of which forms a straight edge; this straight edge being set over the graduation to be copied. Opposite the worker's right hand is fixed the object upon which the scale is to be copied; and as this object is generally a tube, a V groove should be made in the table as shown. The tube or other object on which the scale is to be copied is held down by two parallel rulers, C C'. A bar of light wood about two feet long is held in the two hands as shown; this bar having at the end held in the left hand a steel point which is set into each division of the original or standard scale in succession; the line along the straight edge being, of course, taken. Very good steel scales, divided in millimetres, can now be had at the tool-shops. The end of the wooden bar held in the right hand is furnished with whatever tool is to be used in marking on the object to be graduated. If the object is a burette or a tube $\frac{1}{2}$ inch in diameter.

GRADUATION.

a scratching diamond may be used; and in case when a directly scratched line is allowable, it is the

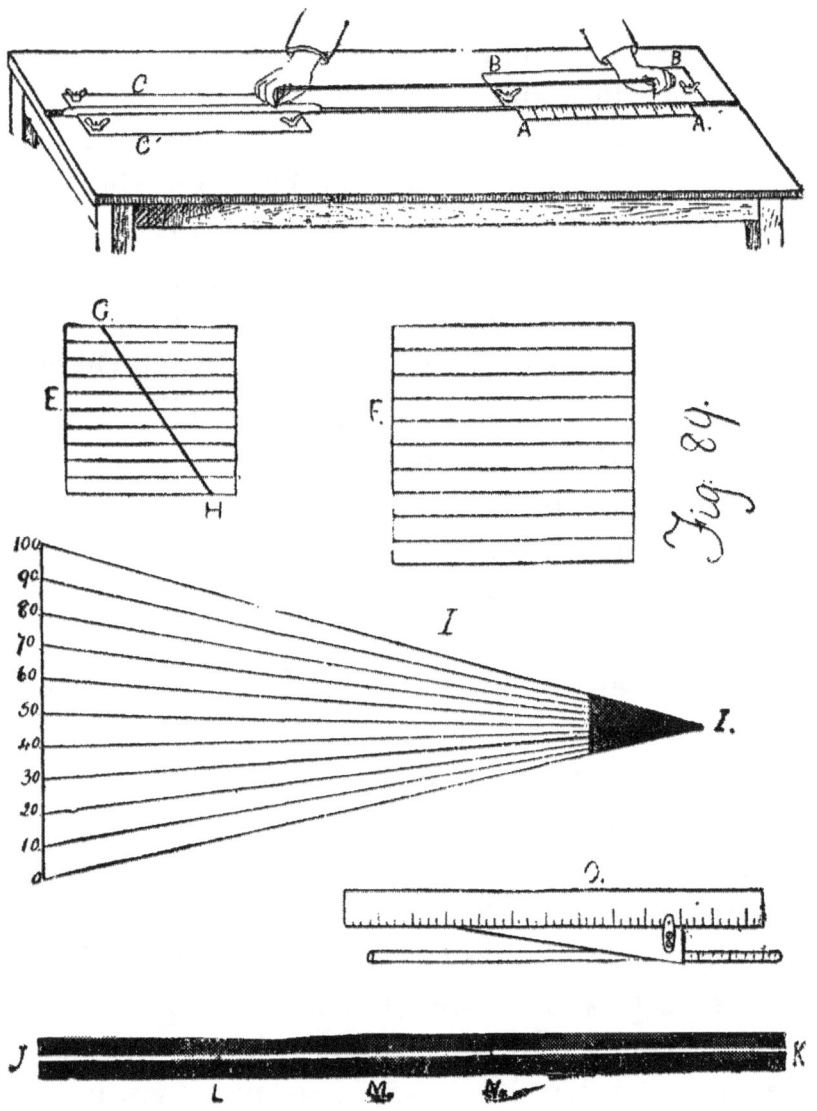

Fig. 84.

best graduation, as it may be made fine or coarse at will, and will hold a black filling better than any etched line. For very fine graduations a worked diamond point may be used, but in most cases the ordinary writing diamond is to be preferred; but before setting the diamond in the divider bar, a direction must be found in which the diamond gives purely a scratch, and this without any tendency to cut or rift the glass (see fig. 58, A and B; also p. 80). If this latter precaution be carefully taken, scratched graduations may be made quite safely on the stem of the chemical thermometer; indeed, I have now in use laboratory thermometers which I so graduated twenty-seven years ago. In using the writing diamond the precaution must be taken to press lightly, otherwise the splinter may wear or alter before the work is finished. When a broad heavy line is required, as on the larger tubes of the burette class, a very much better tool is an old worn and edge-damaged glazier's diamond, such as a pawnbroker will usually sell for about 4s. 6d., but this must be used crossways, so as to plough out a broad groove, which shall contain no element of the true cut or rift. With such an instrument the special caution as to not exercising much pressure is not necessary, as wear tells very little upon it. When etching is to be resorted to, the object must be coated with wax. For this purpose the tube is heated as uniformly as possible to the temperature at which wax melts, and it is then brushed over with melted wax. In order to obtain a uniform coating, the tube should be held horizontally, and rotated until cold. Nothing need be said as to the tool for scraping through the wax ground, excepting that an extremely fine point may give a line which is scarcely visible at first, and which becomes appreciably wider as the graduation proceeds. A worked diamond point may be used, but I think steel is to be preferred, on the whole, for this class of work. When graduation is to be on a strip of paper, as in the case of most hydrometers, an ordinary ruling pen answers well, or a modification of the glass pen described on p. 185 may be employed. At the production of each line between the two straight edges which hold down the object to be divided, the divider bar is used like a beam compasser. It is obvious that each "line" of the graduated scale must necessarily be an arc of a very large circle; but as the ordinary graduation lines on glass articles are short, this is of no moment. The method of ruling lines with the square, mentioned farther on, will theoretically give straight lines, but in practice far worse work is likely to be produced by it than by the method just mentioned. In connection with the length of the lines to be ruled across the article to be graduated, as determined by the distance apart of the clamping rulers, C C, it must be mentioned that in decimal scales it is usual to make every fifth stroke a little longer than the rest. When similar scales are to be made on a number of articles, this extra length of every fifth line can be arranged for by periodical gaps in one of the rulers, C or C'; but in the matter of graduation, I am not writing for the makers of many similar articles, who, as a matter of fact, would not use such an arrangement as I have described. The periodical gap arrangement is quite inapplicable to most of the occasional work to be done with the dividing bar, as in most cases a certain space will have to be divided into (a) a given number of equal lengths; (b) a number of lengths which would be equal were it not for the tapering of the bore of the tube; (c) a number of unequal parts; these being proportional with those on a given scale of unequal parts—as in graduating hydrometers to show specific gravity; (d) as in the previous case, but subject to some correction for the taper of the tube. I have found the following all that could be desired for making the fifth lines (or any others) of extra length when working on a small scale, without expensive dividing machinery. Upon one of the rules C or C′, preferably C′, or that farthest from the operator, is clamped down a clean-cut strip of india-rubber about $\frac{1}{16}$ of an inch thick, and oversailing the rule by as much as is the difference between the long lines and the short lines. For the short lines a gentle bearing is taken against the rubber, and for the long lines sufficient force is used to turn up the strip. In no case (whether rubber strip is used or not) should the side push be taken by the marking tool, but by a rigid stud branching downwards from the dividing bar. *Dividing a line into any required number of equal parts* (case *a*). — A square of thin plate glass, E, fig. 89, is ruled with parallel lines at equal distances apart; this ruling being best done by a ruling machine through a ground of wax, after which the plate is smooth-etched with liquid hydrofluoric acid, as described below. The line to be divided into equal parts is set obliquely across the requisite number of divisions, when it will be divided as required; the line G H, fig. 89, being thus divided into ten parts. One special convenience of the divided glass plate just described is that it can be set at any angle under the straight edge, B B, fig. 89, so that the required divisions can be set off by the dividing bar at once on the article to be divided. In the case of a square plate like E, it is obvious that anything between the unit division and the diagonal of its square can be set off; but it is essential, for general work, to have a range extending not merely from the unit division to the diagonal of its square (1 to the square root of 2), but from unit to double. Instead of attempting to get this by a long and unmanageable plate, it is better to have a second, F, in which the unit is the diagonal of the square on the unit of the first. Such a pair of plates ruled on the basis of 200 millimetres in single millimetres (for E) will serve all ordinary needs; but it is sometimes convenient to have a small portion ruled in half millimetres. I would rather urge the advantages of the glass plate system for making the above-mentioned standard scales of parallel lines, and also the triangular scales for unequal divisions, about to be described; as the fives and tens can be marked in colored lines etched on the under side of the glass, an advantage which will be at once obvious. The reason for my suggestion that the original plate should be thin is, in order that the lines at the back indicating five divisions (filled in with blue), and these indicating ten divisions (filled in with red), shall be easily read in connection with those lines on the face of the plate with which they correspond. *Division of a tapering tube into parts of equal capacity* (case b). — This is a very frequently occurring case; and although the method described below is based on the assumption that the bore of the tube between the points of determination is the frustum of a cone, any required degree of accuracy can be obtained by taking the points of determination near together, and graduating every two reaches, by means of the triangular scale described below; which, like that scale for equal divisions just described, is best etched on a glass plate. The scale, I, consists of a base line graduated into any convenient number of equal parts, and from each graduation a line is ruled to a distant point, I. Any line parallel to the graduated base will be divided in equal parts, but a line drawn unparallel to the base will be unequally divided. The use of this scale is very simple in all cases, and each use of it involves three markings. Take the case of a tube of which the reach L M is equal in capacity to M N, as determined by a thread of mercury or other means, and L N has to be set out into—let us say — 73 parts of equal capacity. From the zero line of the triangular scale to the 73 line, a distance equal to L N is found in which the point M comes to $36\frac{1}{2}$ on the scale. The glass plate being now clamped in position under the bar B B, the selected portion of the scale is set off with the dividing bar as already described. *An enlarged or reduced copying of a standard scale of unequal parts* (case *c*). — This occurs in the case of hydrometers and some other instruments, and if the standard scale is set out on the base of I, fig. 89, any line parallel to the base will give it or any required portion in a reduced form. Case *d*, or the correction for want of cylindricity, together with full data for constructing an original hydrometer scale to show specific gravities according to the method of W. Ackland, is described in the Reports of the Jurors of the International Exhibition of 1851, and is given in quite sufficient abstract in the third volume of **Watts'** *Dictionary of Chemistry*, 1868 ed., p. 206. Instead of using the long table and the dividing bar, a very common way of copying a scale is by fixing the standard rule down on a bench and sliding the long edge of a set square against it, a feeling point resting in each division successively. The divisions are then ruled off on the object to be divided. By clamping a guide bar, such as B B, fig. 89, over one of the glass division plates, and adjusting the feeling point so that it comes close against the guide bar, it becomes possible to adapt this method to the various cases supposed above, but an obvious difficulty is the fact that the object would often have to lie over the glass plate, which would involve troublesome complications in the adjustment of the square. For these and other reasons I recommend the method first described.

Figures and Inscriptions on Graduated Work.—These are, when practicable, most conveniently printed in light skeleton characters; but if written, whether with a diamond point or splinter, or a fluoric ink, such as described on p. 167, no special instructions are required. Printing may be done by several methods. If the original lines were traced through a wax ground for etching, the numbers and letters may be printed through the ground singly from metal type, care being taken that the letters are only warm enough to soften the wax, not warm enough to fuse it. The necessary movement for rolling the metal face of the type against the cylindrical surface is not a difficult one to acquire after a little practice, and if any clearing of the lines is afterwards required, a minute slip of wood moistened with alcohol is the best thing to use, as alcohol will generally penetrate under a very thin film of wax on glass, but will leave a thicker film untouched. Another method of printing is to use the fluoric or etching ink given on p. 167, with rubber-faced type. In any case the writing diamond may be useful for retouching the printed numbers and inscriptions.

Etching Glass.—After the graduations have been made through a wax ground the work should be carefully examined for such defects as are easily remedied at this stage, a false line being readily melted over by a hot wire. Bare places likely to be affected by the etching material should be brushed over with melted wax softened by a little oil of turpentine, as the article cannot be heated at this stage to make the wax flow readily. As a general rule, it is far better to brush the etching material over a graduated scale ruled through wax than to dip the article or to expose it to the vapor of the hydrofluoric acid. The vapor has hitherto been generally preferred, because it gives duller lines than the liquid hydrofluoric acid, but a suitable mixture of hydrochloric acid, fluoride of sodium, and an inert powder such as sulphate of barium, will give a far better dull line etching than the vapor, and it is more uniform in its action and more convenient in many respects. The making of a suitable brush has involved many trials, but I have found a brush constructed as follows to be highly satisfactory. Fig. 90 shows my brush for hydrofluoric acid or mixture containing it. A, B, and C are three thin strips of ebonite, fastened together by two lead rivets as shown, and in the gap formed by B and C the brush proper is fixed, this consisting of seven leaves of vulcanised india-rubber, each about $\frac{1}{32}$ of an inch thick, and made as shown at D. It is convenient to fasten these together at the end, E, with india-rubber cement, so that the brush can be put as a whole into the ebonite handle. A tie round the bifurcated part, B C, with string is sufficient to keep the brush in position; the binding knot shown by fig. 51, C, being convenient. Care must be taken that the acid mixture does not reach the string, and the brush should be taken to pieces and washed after use. If, on the other hand, B C is bound with platinum wire, the brush may be washed after use without

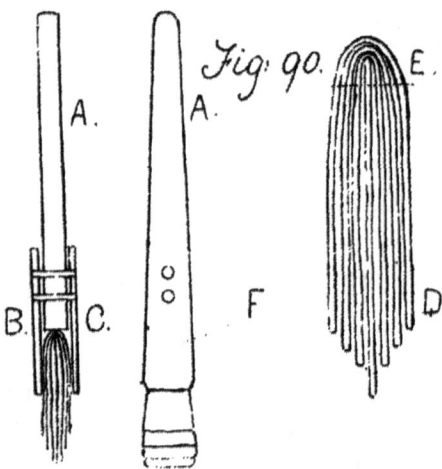

being taken to pieces, or a lead rivet may be passed through at the dotted circle, F. Equal parts of commercial hydrofluoric acid and water may be used with the india-rubber brush, but it is not viscous enough to work well, and gives transparent lines. The following mixture is, however, all that can be desired, and if a little is brushed over the scale ruled on wax, and a very gentle uniform spreading action is kept up for about five minutes, the etching will be finished, after which the article should be well washed with abundance of water and the wax removed. After many experiments the etching mixture which I have found most suitable is that prepared as follows :—

Strong hydrochloric acid, . 1 fluid ounce.
Precipitated sulphate of barium, 120 grains.
Fluoride of sodium, . . 120 ,,

Mix the acid and the sulphate of barium in a leaden vessel, and with a leaden stirrer; then stir in the fluoride of sodium, which should be finely powdered.

Fluoric Inks for Writing and Printing on Glass.—The above mixture is quite unsuited for use as a writing or stamping ink on glass, as the vapor of hydrofluoric acid which is evolved from it would give a halo or nimbus around every character, a fault of all the commercial fluoric inks which I have tried. A good many years ago I prepared a writing ink as follows, and can now recommend nothing better :—

Ammonium fluoride, . . 60 grains.
Precipitated sulphate of barium,. 180 ,,

Grind in a porcelain mortar, and gradually add sufficient water (about $\frac{1}{2}$ oz.) to make a mixture of suitable consistency. When required for use 4 drops of strong sulphuric acid are well mixed with 1 dram ; an egg-cup waxed inside being a convenient vessel, but the unacidified mixture may be kept in a glass bottle. A steel pen may be used, although it corrodes rapidly. The ink is allowed to dry on the surface of the glass, and the longer it remains the deeper is the corrosion. For stamping with rubber-faced type a little more sulphate of barium may be worked into the ink, and some should be uniformly spread on a sheet of rubber. The rubber type should be brought down on this inking slab with such gentle pressure as not to force out the mixture, but merely to divide it between the slab and the glass. Similar care is required in stamping on the glass. An imperfect impression thoroughly wiped off at once does no harm.

Caution as to Hydrofluoric Acid and the above Fluoric Inks.—Persons without a general knowledge of chemistry or those not accustomed to handle corrosive substances should be extremely careful in the use of fluoric etching materials. They should never be allowed to come in contact with the skin, and when washed away an abundant supply of water should be used. The etching ink described on p. 167 gives off vapor of hydrofluoric acid which will slightly corrode neighbouring glass surfaces; hence it should be used in an outhouse or where a draught carries off the vapors. At anyrate, it should never be used near to valuable optical instruments.

A Silicate Ink for Writing or Printing on Glass. —The following silicate ink, if not washed off the glass for some months, will leave an indelible mark, partly owing to the disintegration of the glass surface and partly owing to the deposition of a film of silica on the glass; this silica adhering firmly to the disintegrated surface :—

Syrupy silicate of soda, . . 1 volume.
Caustic soda solution, 10 per cent., 3 volumes.
Indian ink sufficient to make the writing easily visible.

Annealing.—When a thick glass vessel, or a vessel in which there are sudden changes of thickness, is cooled rapidly after the making, it is very likely to break spontaneously. This arises from the fact that the exterior portions in solidifying first so constrain the interior portions that the article is something like a compressed spring, ready to fly as soon as the binding conditions are released. When, however, the object is cooled slowly all the various tensions adjust themselves, and the article is in a more stable condition of equilibrium. A small bulb of glass which is uniformly thin does not require annealing, but in proportion as an article is complex, branched, or irregular in substance, so much greater is the need of annealing. The annealing ovens, fig. 54, A and B, will meet most ordinary needs. If an object heated just short of its softening point is put in the heated oven and the gas is turned down periodically so that the cooling is extended over three or four hours, the annealing will generally be sufficient; but in the case of a lump to form the body of a glass stopcock, fig. 84, C, and p. 146, the time of the gradual cooling should be extended to about twelve hours. Very often a sufficient annealing can be given by laying the object on a bed of finely shredded asbestos (the Italian asbestos being best for this purpose) and covering with the same material. If the asbestos is previously heated, and heated sheets of asbestos millboard are added to still further prevent the rapid escape of heat, so much the better. Hot sand is sometimes used. Newly made articles should never be set down on a rapidly-conducting material. One of the best non-conductive bases for placing hot articles upon is a slab of asbestos millboard upon which a nap has been raised by means of a file card. Covering a hot article with an inverted paper box is a useful expedient for shielding off draughts and somewhat retarding the cooling.

CHAPTER VI.

A FEW EXAMPLES OF SPECIAL ARTICLES FOR LABORATORY OR OTHER USES. THERMOMETERS. VALVES OR THE VALVE SYPHON PRIMED BY BLOWING. A MERCURIAL VACUUM PUMP. BAROMETER-LIKE VACUUM TUBES. LUMINOUS OR PHOSPHORESCENT TUBES. LABORATORY OR OTHER SEALED TUBES. A GLASS PEN AND ITS USES. LENSES. HOLLOW REACTION CELLS FOR MICROSCOPIC OBSERVATION.

Introductory Note.—In planning out the present book my first notion was to make this chapter something like a cyclopædic treatise on the making of special articles for laboratory, technical, and industrial use, but a glance at the enormous mass of notes collected with this view showed that to carry out such an idea would make the chapter five or six times as large as it was practicable to make the whole book. Hence I have rather gone to the other extreme and given very few examples, these being in several cases novel or modified forms. As practically all the important methods and operations have been described in the previous chapter, it might even have been allowable to altogether omit this chapter.

Thermometers.—When a thermometer is to be filled with mercury, a tube having a bore of flat section, like fig. 56, 5–1, 5–$\frac{1}{4}$, is generally used, and ordinarily there is imbedded in the wall of the tube a strip of white enamel glass, to act as a foil to the thread of mercury. The blowing of a bulb, with the precaution desirable in the case of a capillary tube, has already been sufficiently explained, pp. 110 and 104, and for filling the tube a temporary funnel is attached, as shown by fig. 91. To fill the tube with mercury, some of the metal is poured into the funnel and the tube is held over a minute gas flame, which will expand the air, so that some will escape as bubbles through the mercury to the funnel. The bulb being allowed to cool, some mercury will enter —perhaps one-third of the bulb full. The mercury in the bulb is now boiled cautiously, and when threads of mercury, with a short column of air between each, are projected into the tube, the boiling is stopped, and as the bulb cools the mercury in running back will nearly fill it. The boiling is renewed, and this time it is continued until nearly the whole of the mercury is driven out through the tube, and if possible until the last minute column of air is driven up as far as B, a small and rather elongated expansion blown just below the funnel. On now allowing the bulb to cool it may completely fill with mercury, or there may be still a minute globule of air. If so, the globule must be shaken to the top of the bulb, and, by a renewed boiling, be driven

THERMOMETERS.

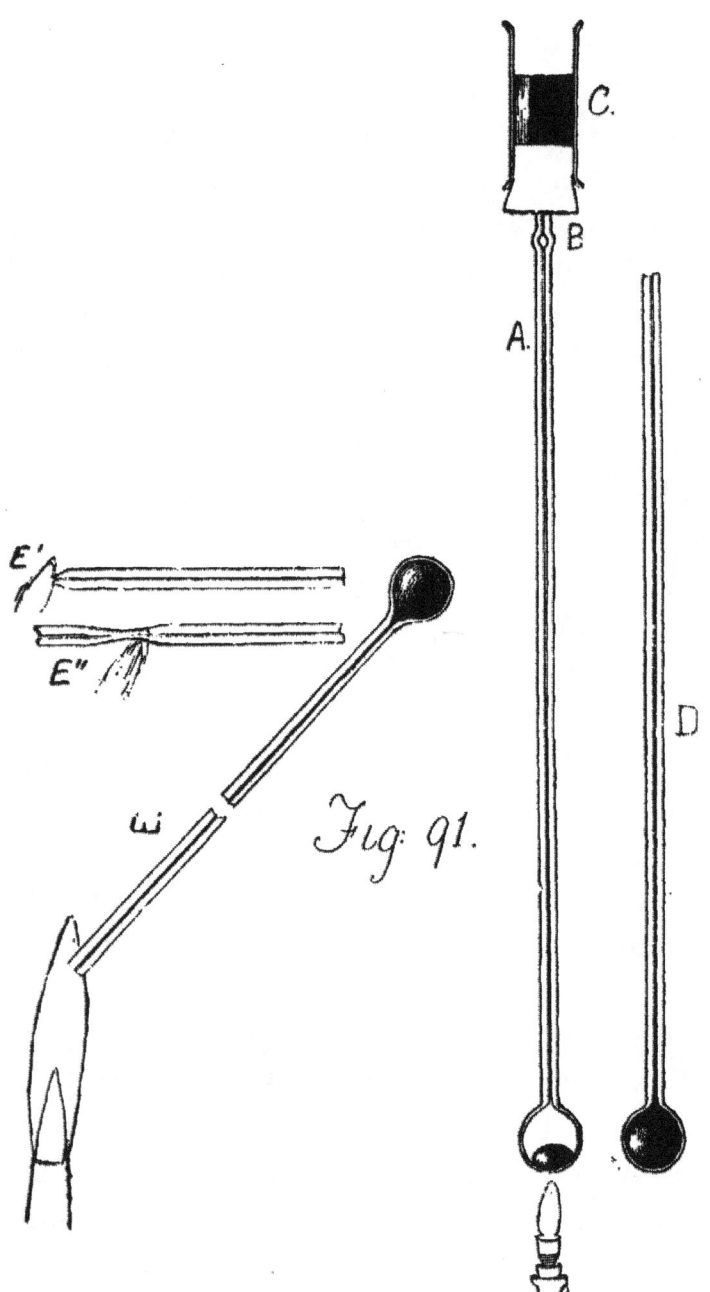

Fig. 91.

upwards and out of the tube. It is at this stage that the small elongated bulb at B often does good service, as the last bubble of air often tends to lodge at the open end of the tube, so as to be redrawn in when contraction takes place, and the same often happens when a large funnel is blown on the end of the tube instead of the movable funnel C. The small elongated bulb B forms a useful trap for the last bubble of air, and, moreover, allows it to be seen, and brought up by a sharp blow on the outside of the tube, if it tends to lodge. The bulb and tube having been filled with mercury, the funnel is removed, and the tube is cut off at a point estimated to give an instrument of the required range, leaving the thermometer, as shown at D. Heat is now applied to the bulb, so as to raise it to a temperature a trifle over that which the instrument is to indicate, and this causes some of the mercury to flow out. While the tube is full of the expanded mercury, or just as the mercury has drawn back for about $\frac{1}{32}$ of an inch, a small blowpipe flame is directed against the cut end, as shown by E, fig. 91, when the end will soften and close, leaving a partial vacuum as the thread of mercury draws back. The softened end can be finished off with a ring or otherwise, as may be desired, the softened glass having no tendency to flow down the capillary tube by the air-pressure. Before sealing, the tube may be drawn to an open point as shown by E'; or it may be drawn out as shown by E'', and sealed as indicated by the sketch.

THE ENCLOSED THERMOMETER. 175

To deal with the various forms of thermometer would involve a special treatise, but the student who has carefully followed the previous chapter and grasped the above should have little difficulty. A few words, may, however, be said as to the construction of the enclosed thermometer, fig. 92, a form now very largely made for dairy and other work, where easy cleaning is a consideration; indeed, this form is perhaps the easiest, quickest, and cheapest to manufacture of all thermometers; the dairy thermometer, graduated to 230° or 240° F., being sold retail for one shilling, and sometimes for less. The bulb is now almost invariably blown from the material of the outer tube, and the fine tube is sealed in by a method which is substantially similar to the method for sealing in a piece for an air-trap, fig. 74, D, and p. 128, but the expansion of the glass of the outer tube is not carried so far as represented by E, fig. 74. The stages are as follows:—fig. 92, B, shows the fine inner tube spread out as shown, by blowing a bulb and opening it, as explained on p. 147; the bent part affording a resting-place for the scale. C shows the inner tube placed in the outer tube; this latter being drawn out as shown, and at this stage it is convenient to steady the thin tube against the outer tube by pushing in a small tuft or mop at the end of a wire. Heat is applied at the bottom until the two glasses have thoroughly united, and by blowing into the piece, as a whole, the lower part is expanded into a bulb, as shown at

176 THERMOMETERS, ETC.

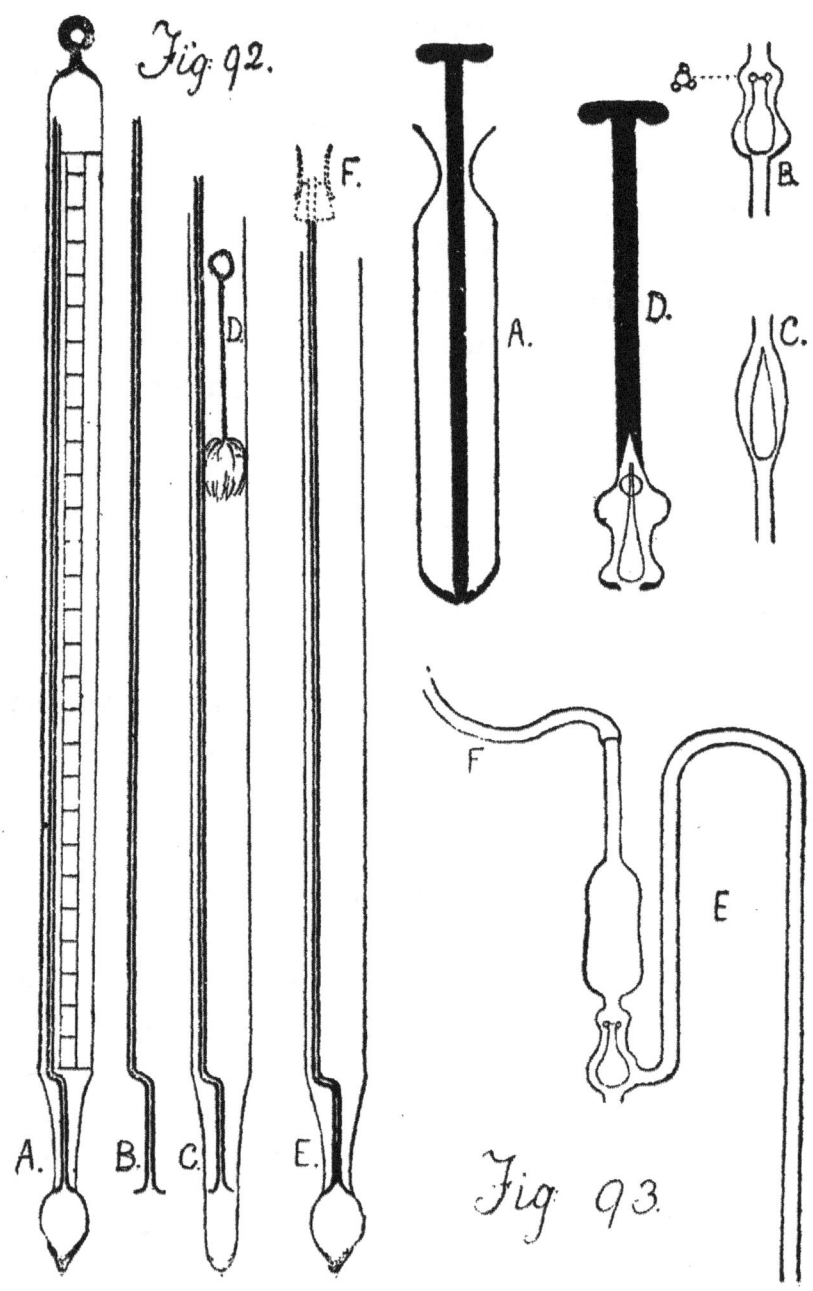

E, but the heat must be so managed as not to unduly expand the part of the outer tube above the bulb. The filling offers no difficulty. For sealing the inner tube, it is usually strained forward, so as not to touch the inside of the outer tube, drawn out fine, by a small pointed flame directed obliquely into the end of the larger tube; when the mercury is brought up to the fine portion, which is now melted off. A small piece of asbestos paper can be laid behind the small tube during this operation, but this precaution is by no means essential. A better way is to pinch off the inner tube at the required depth, by a pair of hard parallel jawed cutting nippers, to bring up the mercury and seal the end by a small flame, as shown at fig. 91, E. The insertion of the scale, whether on paper or other material, requires no special remark, and in sealing the outer tube, the drawing off should obviously be rather as suggested by fig. 66, D, than by E (see p. 103). As regards the ring, see p. 143. In the above notes on the thermometer, I have said nothing about determining the fixed points of the scale, ordinarily the freezing-point and boiling-point of water, as to go thoroughly into this and other matters affecting the accuracy of thermometers would occupy too much space, but as regards graduation the information already given should be ample.

Valves, a Valve Syphon, and a Valve Acid Lifter. —A ground-in valve, made like the stopper of a bottle, but rather more conical, acts fairly well if well covered with a lubricant such as vaseline, but if not so lubricated it is almost sure to jam and fix: this, however, is not the case if one can raise the valve by hand power, as in the acid lifter shown by fig. 93, A; a very convenient form for use with corrosive liquids, or in taking a sample from a barrel. After what has been said as to drawing out (p. 95), thickening an end (p. 98), the syringe handle flat (p. 139), and grinding of stoppers (p. 146), the sketch is sufficient; but I may add a caution to cover the upper part of the stem with paper when grinding the lower part in its seating. This lifter also makes a useful separating funnel for laboratory work. I have sometimes succeeded in making very tight valves in light glass apparatus without grinding, and, moreover, valves which lift with very little pressure, and never stick. Such a valve is shown by B, fig. 93. The spindle is a melted drop on a slightly drawn out stem, and on the top of it three little drops of glass are melted, which prevent the closing of the upper tube when the valve lifts. Both the top and the bottom of the valve chamber must be rounded as shown. In a chamber like C, fig. 93, the valve would be liable to stick fast, either open or closed. A valve in a piston is sufficiently indicated by D, fig. 93. F, fig. 93, shows a form of syphon convenient for acids and corrosive fluids, and which can be primed by blowing through the flexible tube F. After what has been said, its construction should be obvious at the first glance.

A Mercurial Vacuum Pump.—It is desirable to include a sketch of a mercurial pump which is easy to set up, and which will, if tubes and mercury are clean and dry, give the highest vacuum obtainable by this class of apparatus. This pump, shown by fig. 94, is certainly very slow in exhausting, but, as a partial compensation, it is secure against leakage, flow of mercury into the vessel to be exhausted, and catastrophe from the running out of the mercury. For occasional use, a slow pump like this, the tightness and action of which can be depended upon, is very much more useful than any rapid pump with which I am acquainted. The pump is best set up on a wooden partition, the various parts being tied by string to screw eyes; but the horizontal portion of the exhaustion tube, I, should come over a bench. A is a mercury vessel, the exact pattern of which is unimportant: it is connected by a flexible tube with the more special apparatus of the pump. On the flexible tube are two screw clamps, one being set to any special need, and the other being kept for mere opening or closing. The air-trap, C, fig. 94, is made from a tube about 13–10 mm. (see p. 74), and the bulb shown is blown to about double the diameter of the tube. The inflow tube for the mercury, which is lashed to an iron rod resting across the mouth of C, should be about 3–2, and slightly turned up where the inside terminates in the upper half of the bulb. D and E, which may be drawn as one piece from C (see p. 95),

M

should be a little over half a millimetre in external

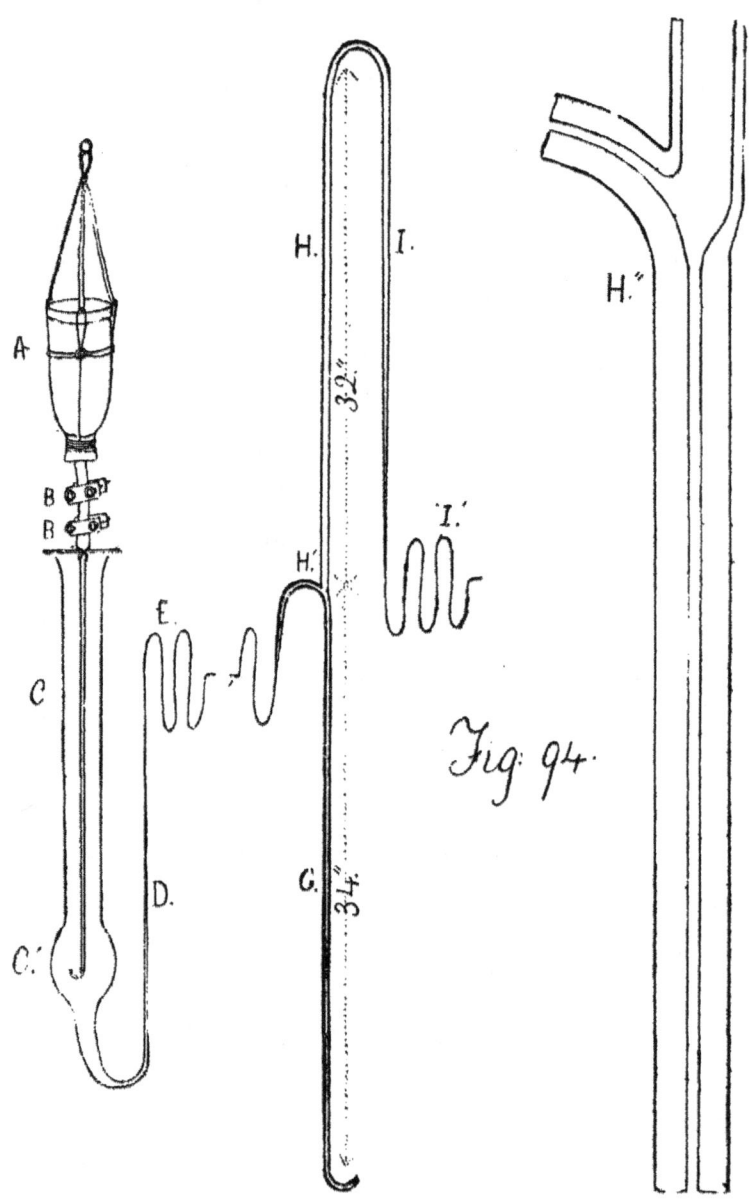

Fig. 94.

diameter, and sealed to the pump proper as explained

on p. 126. The bent fall tube G of the pump is of the special sprengel pump size, 7-1; but the rising portion of the exhaust tube H should be 7-5 (for method of making this joint, see K, fig, 73, and p. 125). The downward portion may be capillary, and its termination is intended for connection by sealing, as explained on p. 126, with the vessel to be exhausted. Note should be made that the rising point of H and also the fall tube below H' are well

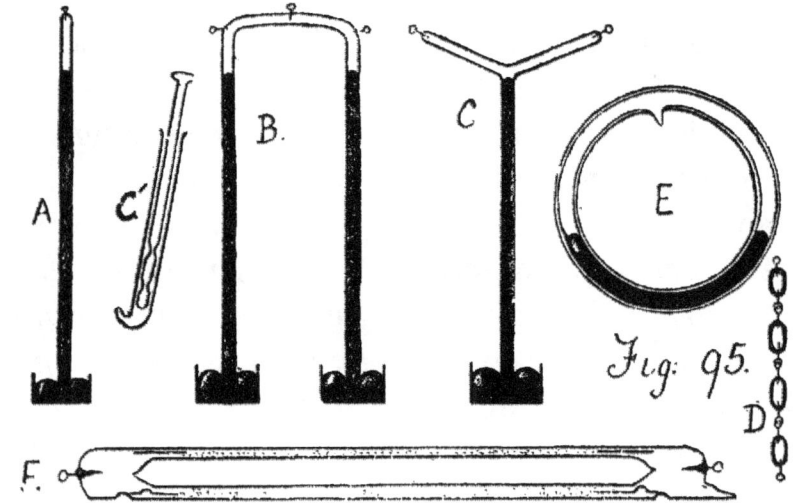

over barometric height, as marked by the braces. The junction at H' is shown full size at H''.

Barometer-like and other Vacuum Tubes.—Now that a renewed interest is being taken in vacuum tubes of all kinds, I may call attention to some more or less novel forms. A, fig. 95, is a barometer tube with a platinum wire electrode at the top, the mercury in the tube serving as the other electrode. B is a double barometer tube with three platinum electrodes, and C is sufficiently explained by the sketch. With such filling as is practicable at the lecture table, it is easy to obtain a sufficiently good vacuum to show stratifications. Small quantities of volatile liquid or gas may be pumped into the barometer tubes by the small syringe C'. At D is shown a chain of minute vacuum tubes like beads, made without exhaustion branch (see p. 151). If these tubes are filled with granular phosphorescent sulphide of calcium (the kind manufactured by W. C. Horne, of Torrens Street, City Road), and the tubes are of uranium glass, an expense of one Watt in electric energy can be made to give a light of two-candle power. A ring-shaped vacuum tube, containing very clean and dry mercury, is shown at E; this being, by preference, made of uranium glass. If put upon a face plate and revolved, a remarkably high return for the energy may be obtained in light; and I cannot but think that this form has a commercial future before it. It will be recognised as a continuous form, founded on the luminous "mercurial mallet" of the older books. It is interesting to note that, under the heading of "mercurial mallet" in Hutton's *Recreations in Mathematics and Natural Philosophy*, vol. iv. p. 155, London, 1803, a suggestion is made for mounting a number on a drum and revolving by machinery, and the following remark is made: "Who knows whether this idea may not enable us, at some future period, to dispense with the candles and lamps which we now employ to light our apartments." The vacuum tube shown by F, fig. 95, contains an inner exhausted tube, and the annulus between this and the outer tube is packed with grains of the before-mentioned phosphorescent or luminous sulphide of calcium.

Sealed Tubes for Preserving Specimens and for Laboratory Uses.—The use of the hermetically sealed tube in past centuries, for the preservation of valuable specimens or relics, has already been referred

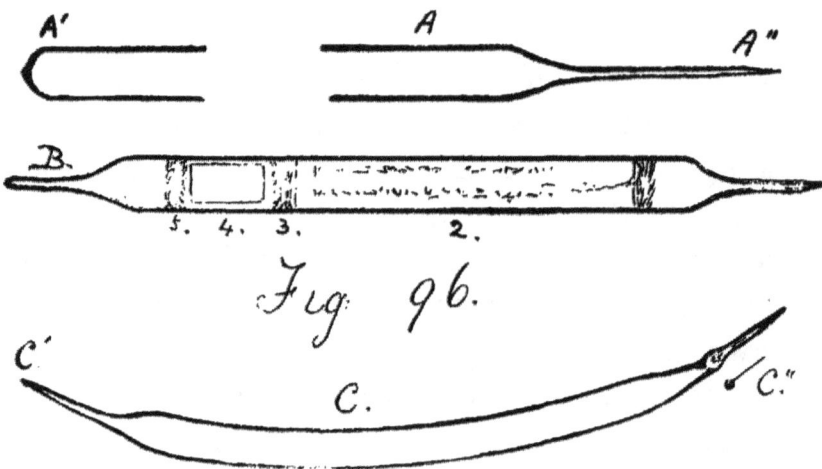

Fig. 96.

to (p. 103); and as it is not unlikely that sealed tubes may be much more largely used than formerly for the preservation of museum specimens, I make the following suggestions. Soft flint glass is, I believe, far more likely to be lasting than the harder glasses, in spite of its tendency to surface corrosion; the frequent disintegration of the harder glasses by rifting and scaling being a far more serious matter. In the case of materials of organic origin, artificial desiccation may be a very great preservative. In this case a tube with two thick drawn out ends (see p. 98) like B, fig. 96, is convenient, and artificially dried air (dried by chloride of calcium or some other absorbent) should be passed through until the object is considered sufficiently desiccated,—this being determinable by weighing the tube occasionally, or by weighing a chloride of calcium tube on the outflow. Assuming the object preserved to be a very tender documentary fragment, or a specimen of a textile material, the arrangement might be something like that shown at B (fig. 96): (1) tuft of asbestos or glass wool; (2) object; (3) tuft; (4) explanatory tablet; (5) tuft. Tubes up to 2 inches in diameter could be worked without difficulty, and this would allow of the display of a surface about 6 inches wide. Laboratory sealed tubes for reactions under heat and pressure should be drawn out to a long thick neck (see p. 98) like A″, fig. 96, and any liquid can be put in after this neck has been drawn out. In opening the tube after the reaction is complete, the extreme point of this neck can be made to project beyond a thick iron plate, serving as a mantlet. The point of a blowpipe flame being directed on the capillary end, it blows out, and any internal pressure is relieved. When a liquid—as obtained by cooling or compressing a gas—is to be sealed under pressure, an arrangement like C is convenient. The liquid being in the curved tube, the small platinum ball obtained by fusing the end of a wire, as shown at C″, is set so as to allow a free way out, and C′ is sealed. The platinum ball being now allowed to fall back to the exit, and a few seconds being allowed for any liquid in the capillary tube beyond it to evaporate, the final seal can be made.

A Glass Pen.—Fig. 96, *bis*, A, shows a form of glass pen having a definite ink-cell at the end, and a capillary point through which a steady flow of ink can take place, and, moreover, a pen very easy to make. The stages are as follows: B, a piece of tube is joined to the rod; C, a hole is blown in the

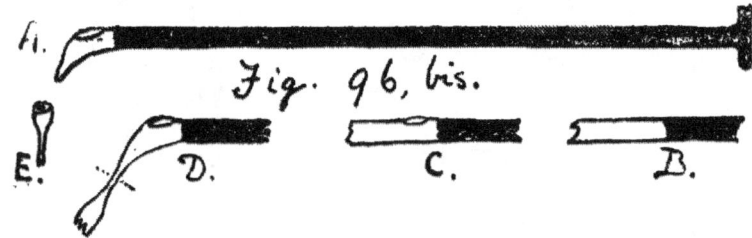

side of the tube; D, the tube is drawn out, and cut off where the size is suitable; E, the edges of the cut off part are slightly rounded at the edge of an ordinary flame. A small funnel-shaped piece, E, corresponding to this pen, is recommended for use with the dividing bar (see p. 159). For rapid writing and some kinds of designers' work, this pen promises to be very useful, as very fine points can be made, or thick-walled and rather fine-bore points, which will give a line of uniform or graduated width nearly $\frac{1}{8}$ inch wide. Mr Scarratt Rigby, the well-known designer of patterns for textiles, was good enough to try some pens which I made, and he has executed the sketch, fig. 97, and the tail-piece, fig. 98 (p. 188), in experimenting with the pens. He says: "I should

All the above, with exception of thickest four parallel lines, drawn with one pen.

Fig. 97. reduced to half the scale of the original.

think such a pen would be admirable for small, quick diagram work, for reproduction, but the drawing I send you does not perhaps fairly represent the capabilities of the pen. You see, it is a new tool, and considerable practice would be required to find out its best points, and show it to the best advantage. For quick dotting and ruling it would, I should think, be unsurpassed. The larger pen is not so handy with Indian ink (which I have used in the drawing), as you will see by the thick lines at the top of the drawing: the ink runs too quickly. I do not know what might be done with a thicker ink, but I should think that with a medium that would give about the right flow it would be very suitable for bolder work."

Bead Lenses; hollow Lens-like Vessels; a Culture Cell for the Microscope.—Bead lenses have already been mentioned; and if the glass is melted in a well formed ring of platinum wire, or in a round hole in a piece of platinum foil held horizontally, a paraboloid lens, defining very well, may be obtained, but flint glass must not be used, as it tends to striæ, which would prevent good definition. Soft german soda glass is satisfactory. For the mode of making ordinary lenses see p. 88. The principle involved in making the hollow lens-like bottles—one of which is shown by fig. 70, N, and the making of which is explained on p. 115—can be applied to the making of a very convenient culture, reaction, or aquarium flask in slide form for the microscope. This is shown in perspective and section by A and B; and after what has been said about joining on branches (p. 124) and making the concave depres-

188   A CULTURE CELL FOR MICROSCOPE.

sions, it will be sufficient to mention here that it is made from tube having a flat section, which can now be obtained as an article of commerce. The two necks shown may be of any pattern, according

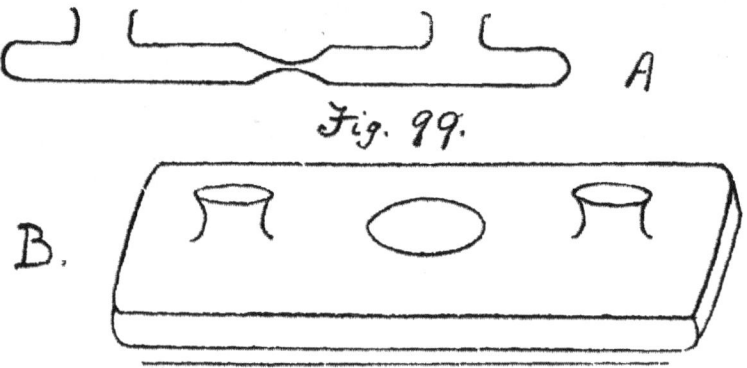

Fig. 99.

to the nature of the work for which the culture cell is to be used. The thinness of the space between the depressions can also be adapted to special requirements.

Fig. 98 reduced to half the scale of the original

CHAPTER VII.

COLORING AND MODIFYING MATERIALS. COLORING IN THE MASS AND FLASHING. GLASS-PAINTERS' FUSIBLE COLORS. COLORING BY CEMENTATION. COBALT. COPPER. MANGANESE. URANIUM. CHROMIUM, ETC.

Coloring in the mass. 'Pot Metal' and 'Flashed.'—Glass is most ordinarily colored by the addition of various substances or compounds of a metallic nature, these being in most cases very intimately incorporated with the materials before melting. One excellent method is to water the sand with the necessary metallic solution, and to dry the sand thus treated. Except in a few cases, the precise nature of the acid element, or the vehicle by which the metal is brought into solution, is a matter of no importance. Glass thus colored is said to be colored in the pot, and an article made from glass so colored is often spoken of as of pot metal, to distinguish it from an article surface-plated with a colored glass, or 'flashed' as it is termed.

Surfacing with a Fusible Colored Glass. Glass-Painting.—If a highly fusible glass is strongly colored, as in the previously mentioned case, then ground to fine powder, mixed with thickened oil of turpentine, painted on a less fusible glass, and cautiously fired, the oil burns out, and the colored glass in melting attaches itself to the less fusible glass. In this process we have the ordinary method of glass-painting. Highly fusible glasses, strongly colored and finely powdered, are known as glass-painters' colors. Such colors may be used (without the oily vehicle) in decorating many small articles made at the blowpipe. The ardent experimentalist will in many cases prepare his own fusible colors (the title of a German handbook on this subject is given in the Bibliography). Manufacturers such as Lacroix of Paris, Hancock of Worcester, or Emery of Burslem, supply potters and glass-painters with such colors in bulk, and the colors of the first mentioned firm may be obtained retail from Lechertier, Barbe, & Co. of Regent Street, London.

Coloring Glass by Cementation or True Staining.—If glass be imbedded in or covered with an inert powder impregnated with copper or silver and the whole is heated to a temperature below the fusing point or even the softening point of the glass, the metal will, under certain conditions, penetrate the glass so as to produce in the former case a red stain and in the latter a yellow stain (almost red when intense). The conditions for the copper-red staining are reducing gases, and for the silver-yellow a volatile haloid of silver—preferably the iodide—is desirable. Coloring by cementation is possible—but not so easy—with a few other metals.

The chief coloring metals are as follows:—

Cobalt.—$\frac{1}{2}$ to 1 per cent. of oxide of cobalt gives an intense blue color.

Copper.—Fully oxidised copper or cupric oxide very easily vitrifies, best with glasses free from lead; 15 per cent. gives a very intense green, and 4 per cent. a very full green. Exposure to reducing gases at once gives a red surface coloration, generally nearly opaque. A cupric oxide glass containing about 12 per cent. of CuO, when very intensely heated and exposed to the action of metallic iron, deposits metallic copper in melted globules; at a somewhat lower heat crystalline spangles are slowly formed, and we obtain the so-called aventurine glass. If the cupric oxide glass contains about 2 per cent. of CuO and a little ferric oxide, it can be brought to an intense ruby color by stirring in the alkaline salt of an organic acid in sufficient quantity to reduce the copper; cream of tartar is used practically. The ruby color thus produced is so intense that the glass can only be used as a plating or flashing, and careful precautions are necessary in working. It is generally assumed that a lightly tinted copper-red glass cannot be prepared and worked, as the reduced copper soon becomes oxidised to the cupric state; but comparatively light tinted red (pot-metal) copper-glasses have been produced, and recently with much success by Herr Putzler of Penzig, Silesia. This glass is said to be made under a patent of Goerish & Co. of Dresden; the reoxidation of the copper being prevented by the solution in the glass of metallic antimony, or perhaps a low oxidation product, which assists in keeping the copper in a state of reduction. This interesting glass is, I find, sold for photographic uses by Mr David Allan of 157 Whitfield Street, Tottenham Court Road. The subject of glasses, both ancient and modern, containing copper is rather one for treating of in a volume than in a paragraph.

Manganese.—Used as binoxide, from 1 to 10 per cent. may be added to any glass, an amethyst color resulting. With the larger proportion the glass appears black, unless the layer is very thin.

Uranium.—2 per cent. gives a fluorescent effect. Sometimes about 1 per cent. of cupric oxide is added to uranium glass, whereby it takes a decided green tint.

Silver.—Half a per cent. gives a clear lemon yellow, but the metal tends to separate.

Iron.—One per cent. in the ferrous state gives a dingy brownish-green. In the ferric state a yellow to orange, but a higher percentage is required for this effect. Highly calcined ferric oxide in a very fusible lead glass behaves like a red pigment without dissolving.

Gold.—$\frac{1}{10}$ of a per cent. gives a pink color, about one per cent. of oxide of tin being a desirable addition. Gold leaf kneaded into glass gives a dull purple.

Platinum and Iridium will give neutral tints ranging to full black, especially with iridium.

Chromium.—Sesqui-oxide of chromium is not very soluble in glasses, but as far as it goes it gives a green tint. Like ferric oxide it may be used as a pigment in soft lead glasses and enamels. Chromic acid may by care be incorporated in glasses free from lead, and it gives a faint brownish-red color. This glass is difficult to work, as reducing gases destroy the color and change it to green. Chromate of lead (chrome yellow) and the basic chromate (chrome yellow) work well in flint glass, giving a lemon tint, which becomes deep orange or red at the softening heat of the glass. In a very soft enamel free from lead chrome red may with care be vitrified as a pigment, but the color is not very lasting, owing to surface disintegration.

Enamels, White Arsenic, Stannic Oxide, Tribasic Phosphate of Lime, Fluor Spar.—These all tend to make glass milk white and semi-opaque, but the arsenic tends very much to fly off in working. Glass made white and opaque is often called enamel, and the same term is commonly extended to all glasses which are made semi-opaque by pigmentary colors or by any other means. Sometimes highly fusible glasses of all kinds are spoken of as enamel, a colorless transparent glass of this sort being sometimes called transparent or crystal enamel.

CHAPTER VIII.

Aging—Disintegration and Decay of Glass—the Devitrifying of Glass.

Action of Moisture of Glass.—Although a glass consisting simply of fused silica (see p. 63) would probably be one of the least alterable of materials, all other glasses are subject to decay and disintegration. Even momentary contact with water removes a trace of the alkali from the surface, and many glasses, if thoroughly ground with water in an agate mortar, lose a large proportion of the alkali in a few hours. Mineral acids have a more powerful action, and by the action of strong hydrochloric acid the highly alkaline glasses, like the soft German glass, may be completely decomposed, silica alone remaining. Such soft alkaline glass loses its alkali rapidly if buried in damp earth, and iridescent scales of silica then cover the surface, this disintegration going quite through the mass in the case of specimens of Roman glass occasionally dug up in the Campagna. Glasses of the soft alkaline character, such as plate glass, soft optical crown, and the German soda glass of the laboratories, often become fissured by innumerable rifts, which can be traced if a powerful beam of light is projected across the glass, and occasionally these rifts are so pronounced as to be immediately obvious to the sight. The alkali of the glass slowly exudes from these rifts, and of such rifted glass—a tube for instance—the surface sometimes scales with an alkaline efflorescence; in other cases a similar action goes through the mass. Such rifted glass is often quite unworkable, and if thick flies to pieces even when cautiously heated. Old samples of soft German tubing which have not yet reached the stage at which rifting can be detected are often so subject to devitrification as to be useless for the purposes of glass-blowing, and therefore the old stock of the dealers should be avoided, and this tendency to devitrification is one reason for preferring flint glass for working at the blowpipe.

Devitrification.—Most kinds of glass, if long exposed to heat at the softening point, become crystalline or fibrous, rough on the surface, and at the same time very hard and less fusible. Glass thus changed is called Reaumur's porcelain, and decorative articles are sometimes converted into it. Scraps or crushings of suitable glass placed in a mould and baked at the softening temperature will agglomerate and devitrify, giving tiles almost as hard as granite. Glass which has been devitrified can be again vitrified by exposure to a considerably higher temperature than its original meeting point; hence it is that, when glass having only a slight tendency to devitrify is worked at the blowpipe, the rough surface, characteristic of devitrified glass, is only observable at the margins of these parts which have been intensely heated. To discuss those chemical conditions which favor and disfavor devitrification would be beyond the scope of the present work, but it may be mentioned that flint glass is so little subject to devitrification that it is rare to find a sample of tubing which shows a trace of this action even in the most prolonged blowpipe operations, or however old the glass may be; still, flint glass is subject to another kind of surface disintegration when worked in the blowpipe, the cause of which I have traced to alternate reduction of lead to the metallic state, and oxidation to litharge.

Pumping Lead out of Flint Glass.—The above mentioned action depends on the fact that when flint glass is blackened by a reducing flame the metallic lead forms a film on the surface, the glass behind the film being less fusible by reason of the subtraction of oxide of lead; and, on oxidising, the film of lead, litharge is formed, and this is extremely fusible, so forms a very fluid layer. Unequal surface tension is thus set up and the glass drifts into a spotted condition of unequal thickness, often accompanied by a little true devitrification by reason of the removal of lead from certain portions. If flint glass is subjected to a considerable reduction, so that much lead is removed, the remainder often devitrifies, giving a black, infusible, and unmanageable mass. The practical lesson is to so work the glass that blackening does not take place (see p. 25), as flint glass once blackened at the blowpipe cannot be restored to its pristine condition.

Changes in Colored Glass.—Many colored glasses change color slightly on exposure to light, and glass painting executed with highly fusible glass-painters' colors (see p. 190) is very liable to disintegrate; therefore one must not look upon stained glass works as absolutely permanent, although they take a position so much higher than paintings on paper or canvas as to stand in altogether a different category. As an example of change, glass containing manganese may be mentioned. When the quantity is small and the metal is not fully oxidised, scarcely any color is imparted, but such glass gradually becomes violet by the action of air and light. In old times plate glass frequently contained enough manganese in the reduced condition to cause the glass to become distinctly violet on exposure to air and light.

CHAPTER IX.

FANCY AND DECORATIVE ARTICLES MADE AT THE BLOWPIPE.

ENDLESS variety of style and coloring can be easily realised in working at the blowpipe, and the fundamental means by which the various effects are to be produced have already been explained. The colored frontispiece plate, fig. 100, and the key to it, fig. 101, will afford many suggestions, and the following notes on some of the examples should be quite sufficient to serve as suggestions for the technical side of the question. As regards the artistic side, I take it there is but one canon, and that is for the workman to do that which pleases him at the moment. It is only in this way that free and unfettered fine art can manifest itself, all attempts to do that which others say should be done and all attempts to follow any convention being inimical to artistic manifestations. In other words, I take it that only the technics which surround fine art can be taught. Following this view, I have included in the colored sheet only the simplest forms, and these are the result, not of plastic manipulation, but rather of allowing natural forces to assert themselves; they are shapes into which the glass tends to fall and draw when natural forces are allowed free play in certain directions. Those who have artistic aspirations in the sense of using the blowpipe flame as a modelling tool—a tool acting with equal facility for relief or intaglio—will find ample suggestions on p. 111 to p. 114 to enable them to model figures, faces and expressions, as Venetian artists did in times gone by.

Notes on Colored Plate, fig. 100—The Numbers refer to the Key Plate, fig. 101.—No. 1: The neck of the bottle is made by laying a short strip of white enamel glass longitudinally on a tube about $13-11\frac{1}{2}$, drawing out as shown by fig. 65, S, T, or V (see also p. 100), and twisting during the drawing out, this being cut off. A ball of mixed colored glasses is melted on the end (see p. 107), and this is blown out. The feet are from the same mass, and for details see p. 138. No. 2: This is from a piece of tube about $13-11\frac{1}{2}$, but having in its substance a white strip, this tube being sold for making graduated burettes. In drawing out the neck part, the tube is twisted; other operations as in stages A to E, fig. 70, except that at the stage A the soft body is rolled in a powdered green enamel. The bottom is not flattened quite like E, but by re-heating and bringing down steadily and vertically on a tile. No. 3: The neck and body as in the last case, but from plain tube, and not twisted. At stage A, fig. 70, the soft glass is rolled over a strip of gold leaf laid on a piece of asbestos millboard. The gold breaks up into minute patches in the blowing out. Foot as

200 DECORATIVE STYLES.

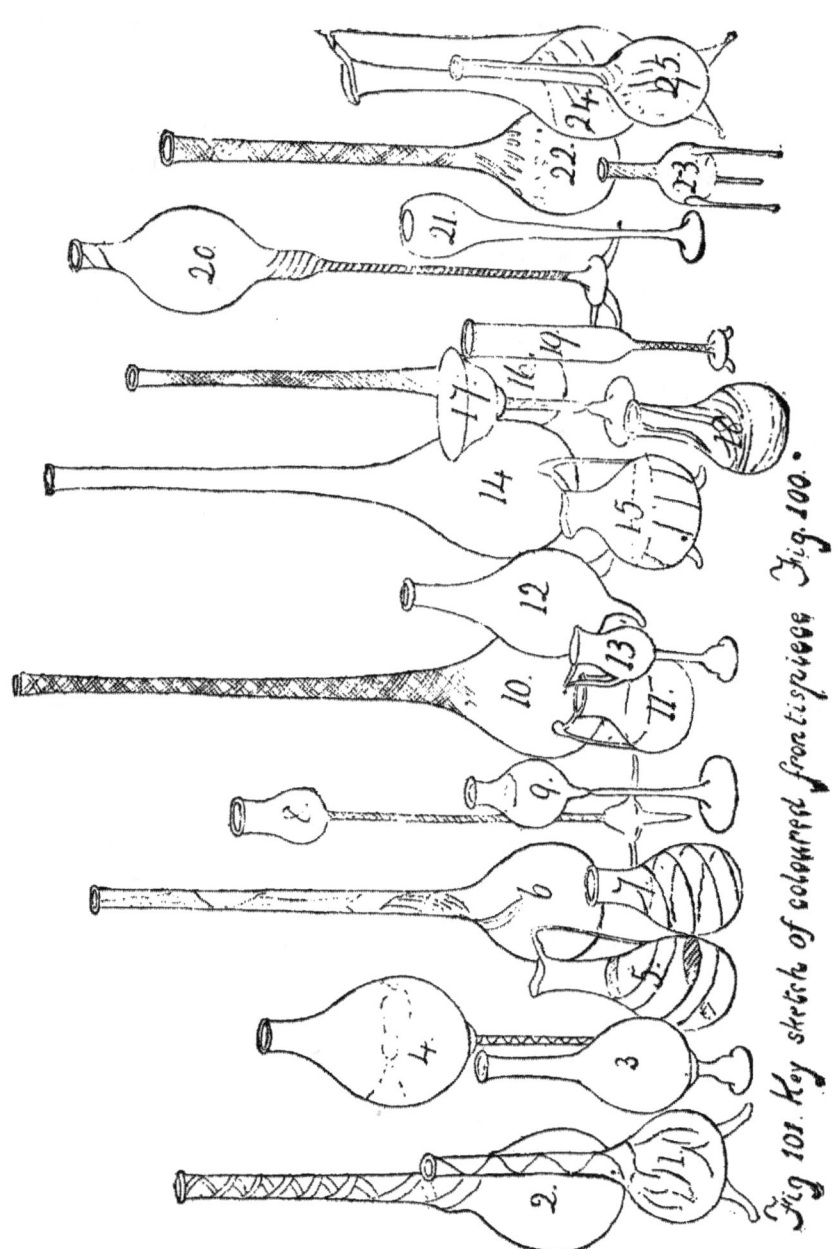

Fig. 101. Key sketch of coloured frontispiece Fig. 100.

explained on p. 138. No. 4: Round the end of a piece of tube about 13–11½ are melted alternate patches of green and amethyst glass, these forming a rough continuation of the tube; another similar tube is joined on, a neck is drawn out and the tube is sealed, so that the ring of colored windows comes equatorially on such a piece as A, fig. 70. The piece is then blown out. To make the spiral stem a thread of black (deep amethyst) glass is placed in the bore of a tube, 7–1, a lump is melted at the end, as shown by fig. 62, E; this is attached to the previously heated bottom of the bulb, and as pulled out it is twisted. Footbell form with branches, fig. 81, F (see also p. 140). No. 5: Round a bulb at stage A, fig. 70, a thread of orange glass is wrapped, bulb blown and flattened at bottom as No. 2. The spout is formed by one outward pressure with carbon turnpin. Handle as explained on p. 141. No. 6: A thread drawn as a composite spiral of black and blue enamel glass is wrapped round a tube about 13–11½, and this part is drawn out with twisting to form neck. Bulb like No. 2, but plain. No. 7: Similar to No. 5, but two threads of different glasses, and finished with plain neck (see p. 93). No. 8: Body from white enamel glass tube, made like No. 3, stem from mass like F, fig. 62, but partly of blue enamel glass and partly of colored glass, attached and twisted in withdrawal as in case of No. 4. Foot similar to No. 4. No. 9: Body of a fluorescent blue glass; above descriptions cover remainder. No.

10 : Generally similar to No. 6, but before drawing out, the portion of the tube forming the neck was studded with numerous small patches of enamel glass; twisted in drawing out neck. No. 11: Similar to No. 5, but plain body of fluorescent blue glass. No. 12: Plain bulb of yellow glass, with feet of white enamel glass (see p. 138). No. 13: Similar to No. 11, but of white enamel glass on foot, fig. 81, B (p. 139). No. 14: Of gold pink glass, similar to No. 2, but plain. No. 15: Similar to No. 11, but body from composite tube of white and blue enamel made as described on p. 134. No. 16: Similar to No. 10, but complex spiral changes from black to blue, and again to black. The small dots of glass which form the spiral when the neck is drawn out and twisted, are placed almost in contact on the large tube, and in the heating they run together, so that unbroken twisted threads changing from color to color appear on the neck. No. 17: Vase made by trimming bulb with scissors, as described on p. 84. Stem similar to that of No. 4, but with white twisted thread. Foot like that of No. 3. No. 18: Bottle like Roman tear bottle, made entirely of fragments of glass mixed together. Mass blown to bulb, as described on p. 107. Elongated as shown in fig. 77. Bulb blown on end of D, fig. 77, and cut from the tube serving as a blowing cane. No. 19: From white enamel tube, spiral stem as No. 17. Foot, a syringe handle flat (see p. 139) with three spurs. No. 20: Bulb is from a drawing out

like S′, T, or V, fig. 65. Spirals as in case of Nos. 10 and 16, but black. Foot like No. 4. No. 21: Inverted bulb of gold pink glass, hole at top blown as explained on p. 116. Foot like No. 9. No. 22: As No. 10, but the dots of enamel glass which form the spirals are continued down to bulb, where some are shown but slightly extended and twisted. No. 23: Bulb with spiral threads in two colors on neck. Feet like those of fig. 1, but commencing higher up and drawn down straight. No. 24: Neck and bulb drawn from a composite tube made from blue and white enamel rods, the body being of same piece, but mixed. Feet like those of No. 1, but unmixed white enamel. No. 25: Plain neck and handle, body of composite tube, like No. 24, but of blue and amethyst.

Hitherto tubes and rods of colored glass suited for decorative work have been somewhat difficult to obtain in small quantities, as glass manufacturers will seldom trouble themselves with orders for less than several hundredweight; but, as I am passing the last sheets through the press, Messrs Becker & Co., laboratory furnishers, of 33, 35, and 37 Hatton Wall, London, say that they are making arrangements to stock various colored tubes and rods, and of a quality of glass which will work with their ordinary colorless soft German soda glass as supplied for laboratory use. They also keep in stock the blowpipe tables and other manufactures of M. Enfer (see p. 48).

CHAPTER X.

Glass-Making at the Blowpipe and on a Laboratory Scale.

If the materials for glass-making are in a very fine state of division and thoroughly mixed by sifting, small globules of glass may be made in rapid succession before the blowpipe in a ring on a piece of platinum wire. A, fig. 102, represents a convenient wire loop of the actual size, and it is convenient to fuse the platinum wire into a glass handle, A'. The information already given in Chapter IV. and Chapter VII. will afford sufficient information as to the composition of plain and colored glasses to enable an experimenter to make a beginning at any rate. The silica should not be taken as sand, but as very fine ground or precipitated silica, both of which can be obtained from operative chemists—Messrs Hopkin & Williams, 16 Cross Street, Hatton Garden, London, for example. The wire-loop, having been heated to redness, is dipped in the mixture, again heated, and the operations are repeated until as much has been gathered as the loop will hold. After thorough fusion the drop is intensely heated and allowed to flow off. The globules thus made can be gathered and blown, as explained on p. 107.

GLASS MAKING ON SMALL SCALE. 205

For work on a rather larger scale a small crucible may be enclosed in a double circulation fire-clay crucible jacket, such as is shown in section by fig. 103 (sold by Gallenkamp & Co., of 19 and 21 Sun

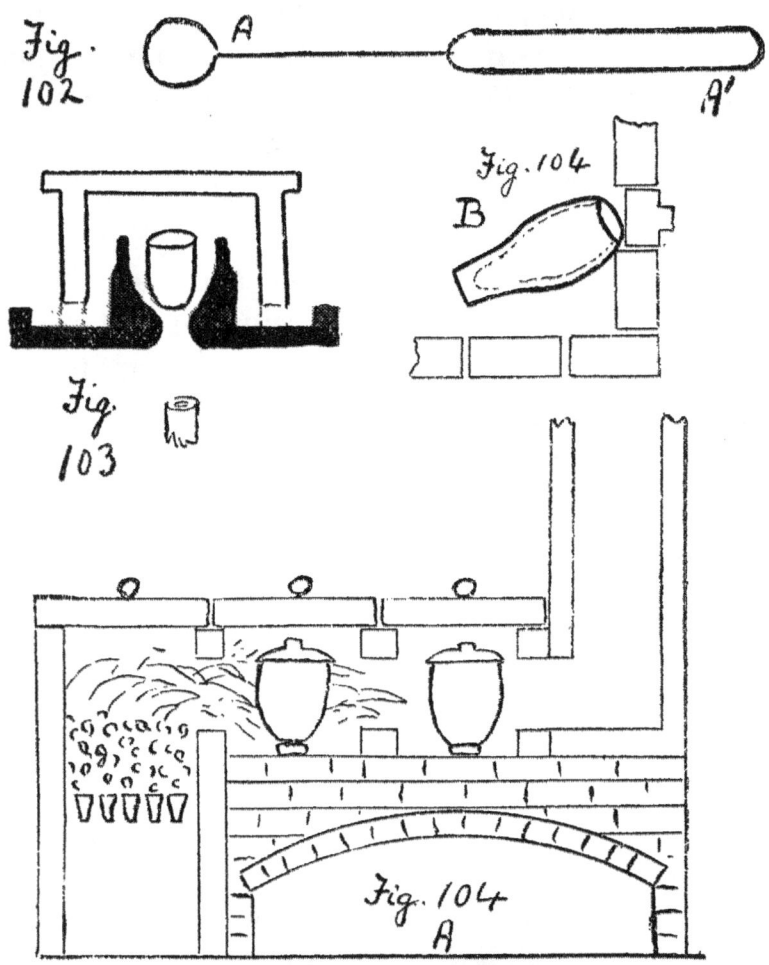

Street, Finsbury Square, E.C.), and heated by the blowpipe, while for still larger quantities a small reverberatory furnace, as shown in section by fig. 104, may be built. When flint glass is being made, the contents of the crucible must not be exposed to furnace gases; the long crucible called a skittle-pot, mounted as shown by fig. 104, is convenient.

By using a piece of iron pipe ($\frac{1}{4}$ inch gas barrel) as a blowing cane, a bulb can be blown and drawn into tube, as explained on p. 131. From the point of view of color and decorative effect, it is a great advantage for an experimenter to make a stock of tubes for himself. If a silver yellow glass, a cobalt blue glass, a gold pink glass, and a colorless glass, are set out in separate pots in a furnace such as fig. 104, tubes or articles of almost any required tint may be made. With the blowing tube successive dips are taken in the several pots; the colors and the plain glass being thus layered upon each other in any required proportion. On p. 132 will be found instructions for making tubes.

CHAPTER XI.

THE BIBLIOGRAPHY OF GLASS.

THE following short list embodies a few works which are either of interest from their intrinsic or historical importance, or from their ready accessibility. Most of them can be seen at the Patent Office Free Library, Southampton Buildings, Chancery Lane, London, which is open till 10 o'clock in the evening all days, except Sundays and public holidays.

1662. C. MERRET. The Art of Making Glass. London. Reprint, 1826, by Sir T. Phillips.
1689. KUNCKELN. Ars Vitraria Experimentalis, 2 vols., 472 pp. Frankfort and Leipzig. C. Riegels.
1752. Art de la Verrerie de Neri, Merret et Kunckel, 430 pp. Paris.
1774. LE VILLE. L'art de la Peinture sur Verre et de la Vitrerie, 245 pp. and 13 pls. in the Folio Cyclopædia, "Arts et Metiers." Paris.
1785. J. KUNCKELN. Volstandige Glassmacher Kunst. (reprint). Nuremburg.
1800. C. LOYSEL. Essai sur L'art de la Verrerie. Paris.
1832. D. LARDNER. Porcelain and Glass, 334 pp. London. Longman.
1849. APSLEY PELLATT. Curiosities of Glass Making. London.
1863. P. FLAMM. Le Verrier du xix Siècle. Paris. E. Lacroix.
1868. G. BONTEMPS. Guide du Verrier, 774 pp.

Paris. Libraire du Dictionaire des Arts et Manufactures.

1877. E. PELIGOT. Le Verre. Paris. 495 pp. G. Masson.

1878. A. NESBITT. Glass. A South Kensington Art Handbook. London. Printed for the Committee of Council on Education, Chapman & Hall, 193 Piccadilly. 8vo, 318 pp.

1881. N. GRÆGER. Handbuch der Glass Fabrikation. 8vo, 318 pp. Weimar. B. T. Voigt.

1885 (about, no date in book). M. A. WALLACE-DUNLOP. Glass in the Old World, 272 pp. London. Field & Tuer.

1885. F. MILLER. Glass Painting, 116 pp. London. Wyman.

1885. GERSBACH. L'art de la Verrerie. Paris. Maison Quantin.

1886. W. A. SHENSTONE. Methods of Glass-Blowing, for Physical and Chemical Students, 86 pp. London. Rivingtons.

1888. MAX MULLER. Die Fabrikation der fur die Glassmalerei, Emailmaleri und Porclainmalerie geeigneten Farben. 8vo, 140 pp. Weimar. B. F. Voigt.

1889. W. MERTENS. Die Fabrikation und Raffinirung des Glases. Vienna, Pest, and Leipzig, 390 pp. A. Hartleben's Verlag.

1892. F. FISCHER. Die Kunst der Glass Masse Arbeitung, 139 pp. Vienna, Pest, and Leipzig. Hartleben.

1894. Abridgements of Specifications, Class 26, Glass, 1877 to 1883. 1s. Patent Office, London.

1894. APPERT ET HENRIVAUX. Verre et Verrerie. Paris. Gauthier Villars.

1894. G. S. RAM. The Incandescent Lamp and its Manufacture. London. Electrician Printing and Publishing Co.

1895. DJAKONOW UND LERMANTOFF. Die Bearbeitung des Glasses auf dem Blasetisch, 154 pp. Berlin. Friedländer.

1896. E. GARNIER. Histoire de la Verrerie, 574 pp. Tour. Mame et Fils.

1896. Abridgements of Specifications, Class 56, Glass, 1884 to 1888. 1s. Patent Office, London.

1897. R. GERNER. Die Glas-Fabrikation, 348 pp. Vienna, Pest, and Leipzig. Hartleben.

1897. A. HARTSHORNE. Old English Glasses. London and New York. Arnold.

CHAPTER XII.

INDEX.

ACID lifter, 176, 178.
Air spiral, 135.
Air-traps and internal sealings, 128.
Allan, D., 192.
Alexandrian glass-houses, 15.
Animal forms, modelling, 114.
Annealing, 169.
Annealing ovens, 61.
Appert and Henrivaux, 208.
Aquarium cell, 187.
Aventurine glass, 191.

BECKER & Co., 203.
Bellows, Egyptian, 13, 14.
Bellows, various, 41–51.
Bending, 118.
Bibliography of glass, 207.
Blowpipes, 21–37.
Blowpipe flame, Criteria of, 23.
Bohemian glass, 64.
Bontemps, G., 207.
Branching and joining, 120–127.
  ,,   clamp, 59.
Bulbs, 104–111.
  ,, shaping and modelling, 111–115.

CALLENDAR, Mr H. L., 63.
Callipers, 58.
Castaldi, 150.
Cementation, 190.
Claws, feet, and flats, 139.
Closing an end, 101.
Cobalt, 191.
Colored glasses, 189.
  ,, glass, alteration of, 197.
  ,, ,, composite, 205.
  ,, plate of examples, 2.
Contents, 4.
Contracting, 93.
Copper, 191.
Crookes, 9.

Crown glass, 65.
Crushing or powdering glass, 137.
Culture cell, 187.
Cutting glass, 78–85.
  ,, tools, etc., 53–57.

DECORATIVE articles, 198.
Devitrification, 195.
Djakonow and Lermantoff, 208.
Drawing out glass, 95.
Drilling, 86.

EDUCATIONAL aspect, 9.
Egyptian methods, 13.
Electrodes, 150.
Enamels, 69, 193.
Enfer, M., 47, 203.
Etching, 165–168.
Eyes, handles, and rings, 141.

FEET, claws, and flats, 139.
Figures and inscriptions, 164.
File, 53.
Filing glass, 85.
Fischer, F., 208.
Flam, P., 207.
Flame, 20.
Flashing, 136, 189.
Flats, syringe handle, 139.
Flint glass, 25, 66, 196.
Funnel, thistle, 147.
Furnaces for glass-making, 205.
Fusible glasses, 69.

GALLENKAMP, 205.
Garnier, E., 209.
Gas furnace, 32, 205.
Gerner, R., 209.
Gersbach, 208.
Gimmingham, Mr, 33.
Glass-blowers at work, 6.
Glass-painters' colors, 190, 208.

Gœrish & Co., 191.
Gold, 192.
Graduation, 155-166.
Graeger, N., 208.
Griffin, J. J., 32.
Grinding, 84-85, 146.
    „   pistons, etc., 143.
Guaging rods or tubes, 74.

HANCOCK (of Worcester), 190.
Handles, rings, and eyes, 141.
Hartshorne, A., 209.
Hebrew glass, 14, 16.
Henrivaux. *See* Appert.
Hermes (of Alexandria), 103.
Holes in glass, 86, 87, 115-118.
Holy Crown, the, 104.
Home work, 7.
Hopkin and Williams, 240.
Hutton's mathematics, 182.
Hydrometic scales, 163.

INCANDESCENT LAMP, 151, 153, 208.
Internal sealings and air-traps, 129.
Iridium, 192.
Iron, 192.

JENA glasses, 67.
Joining and branching, 120-127.

KNIVES, 53.
Kunckeln, 6, 7, 207.

LACROIX, M., 190.
Lamps for oil, etc., 37-40.
Lamp, Incandescent, 151, 153, 208.
Leading cracks, 56.
Lechertier, Barbe & Co., 190.
Lermantoff. *See* Djakonow.
Lenses, 88, 187.
Le Ville, 207.
Lifter for acids, 176, 178.
Light for working, 52.
Louis IX., 18.
Loysel, C., 207.

MAKING glass on small scale, 204.
Manganese, 67, 192, 197.
Mercurial pump, 179.
Merrits, C., 207.
Mertens, W., 208.

Metal fittings, connecting to, **154**.
Middlesex County Council, **3, 5,** 11.
Miller, F., 208.
Modelling animal and other forms, 114.
Moisture, action on glass, 194.
Moulding, 148.
Mouthing, 93, 94.
Muller, Max, 208.

NEGRETTI AND ZAMBRA, 9.
Neri, 8.
Nesbitt, A., 208.

ORIGIN of glass, 12.

PALISSY, BERNARD, 16.
Parnell, E. A., 18.
Peligot, E., 208.
Pellatt, Apsley, 207.
Pen, a glass, 185.
Perforation, 86, 87, 115-118, 147.
Phosphorescent material, 182.
Pistons, fitting and grinding, 143.
Piston with valve, 176, 178.
Plate glass, 65.
Platinum, 150, 192.
Pliny's story as to origin, 16.
Polishing, 88.
Pot metal, 189.
Powdering or crushing glass, 137.
Preface, 5.
Pressing, 148.
Printing types, 150.
Putzler, Herr, 191.

RADIATORS, 57.
Ram, G. S., 208.
Rapid change blowpipe, 34.
    „   of jets, 23.
Recent progress, 18.
Rigby, Mr Scarratt, 185.
Rings, handles, and eyes, 141.
Rods and tubes composite, 135.
    „   making, 132.
Roman glass, 16, 194.
Ruby glasses, 191.

SCALES, graduated, 155-166.
Sealed tubes, 103, 183.

Seals and gems, 149.
Schott, Herr, 68.
School for glass-working, 19.
Shanking or crushing, 85.
Shanks, 59.
Shenstone, W. A., 208.
Silica (pure) as glass, 63.
Silver, 192.
Smith's metal warehouse (Clerkenwell), 28.
Specifications, 208, 209.
Spiral of air, 135.
Spirals, 119.
Sprengel pump, 179.
Spun glass, 137.
Staining, 190.
St Louis, 18.
Stopcocks, 146.
Stoppers, 146.
Strabo, 15.
Syphon, 176, 178.
Syringe handle flats, 139.
  ,,   thickened nose, 96, 99.
  ,,   without packing, 143.

TECHNICAL Education, 5, 11.
Thermometers, 172–176.
  ,,   glass for, 68.
Thickening, 95, 98.
Thistle funnel, 147.
Threads, 137.
Tongs, 58.
True Cross, the, 103.
Tubes, 70–77, 131.
  ,, cleaning, 76.
  ,, gauging, 71–77.
  ,, and rods, composite, 135.
  ,,   ,, making, 131.
Turn pins, 58.
Types, glass, 150.

URANIUM, 182, 192.

VACUUM tubes, 181.
Valves, 177.
Venetian glass, 17.

WALLACE DUNLOP, Mr. 104. 208.
Writing on glass, 167.

Recipes
for
Flint Glass Making

By a
British Glass Master and Mixer

BEING LEAVES FROM THE MIXING BOOK OF SEVERAL
EXPERTS IN THE FLINT GLASS TRADE

CONTAINING UP-TO-DATE RECIPES AND VALUABLE INFORMATION
AS TO CRYSTAL, DEMI-CRYSTAL AND COLOURED GLASS
IN ITS MANY VARIETIES

IT CONTAINS THE RECIPES FOR CHEAP METAL SUITED TO PRESSING,
BLOWING, ETC., AS WELL AS THE MOST COSTLY CRYSTAL AND RUBY

BRITISH MANUFACTURERS HAVE KEPT UP THE QUALITY OF THIS
GLASS FROM THE ARRIVAL OF THE VENETIANS TO HUNGRY
HILL, STOURBRIDGE, UP TO THE PRESENT TIME

THE BOOK ALSO CONTAINS REMARKS AS TO THE RESULT OF THE METAL
AS IT LEFT THE POTS BY THE RESPECTIVE METAL MIXERS, TAKEN
FROM THEIR OWN MEMORANDA UPON THE ORIGINALS

SECOND EDITION

"THE POTTERY GAZETTE" OFFICES
8 BROADWAY, LUDGATE HILL, E.C.

1907

First Edition, *July*, 1900.
Reprinted, *April*, 1907.

CONTENTS.

	PAGE
Notes by the Compiler	iii
Ruby Glass Recipes	1-5
German Metal Recipe	6
Cornelian Recipes	7
Sapphire Blue Recipes	8
Crysophis Recipes	9
Opal Recipes	10-13
Turquoise Blue Recipes	14, 15
Gold Colour Recipes	16
Green Recipes	17
Malachite Recipes	18
Black Recipe	19
Canary Recipes	19
White Opaque Glass Recipes	20
Sealing Wax Red Recipes	21
Flint Glass Recipes	22-25
Achromatic Glass Recipe	26
Paste Glass Recipe	26
White Enamel Recipe	27
Firestone Recipe	27
Dead White Recipe	28
Agate Recipes	28
Canary Recipes	29
Index	30

NOTES BY THE COMPILER.

Repeats are given of more than one recipe, so that the mixer may acquaint himself how to use up his cullet or to vary his mixture to suit his requirements.

The cost given of the cheap metal is based on the cost of materials some year or two ago, but it is approximately correct at the present time.

The sand used in most of the recipes is French (Fontenbleu), except in some old forms, when it was Isle of Wight; and the soda supplied by a Northwich firm.

Colouring should generally be about half put into the batch and the other half reserved until the long proof has been taken off, when it can be added to or diminished to suit furnace or the weather.

The sand in the *crystal* should be washed and calcined. In the commoner metal it is used as it arrives; still the quality is greatly improved by the first process.

Many of the finest colours containing cryolite should be worked immediately it is plain.

In using brass, it is necessary to insure correctness that it should always be the same. Brass differs in its composition.

The greatest care should be taken in the purity of all material, and the greatest care should be taken that everything is clean and free from dust and dirt.

In all these colourings allowance must be made throughout this book for the state of the furnace, weather, purity of sand and material, etc.

July, 1900.

RUBY.

	Cwt.	qrs.	lb.	oz.
French Sand (Fontenbleu)	2	2	20	0
Red Lead	2	2	20	0
Saltpetre	0	0	18	0
Antimony	0	0	9	0
Manganese	0	0	2	0
Gold in Solution, " Purple Precipitate of Cassius"	0	0	0	1½
Nitric Acid	0	0	0	1
Muriatic Acid	0	0	0	4

"Mix and then add the gold; when fine, work into lumps. There used to be much difficulty in preparing this purple precipitate, but it is now an article of commerce. Mind it is pure."

ANOTHER RUBY.

Sand	32 lb.
Red Lead	36 ,,
Saltpetre	16 ,,
Manganese	1¾ oz.
Antimony	2 ,,
Gold (in Solution)	1 ,,

ANOTHER RUBY.

Saltpetre	9½ lb.
Sand	18 ,,
Red Lead	23 ,,
Red Lump Cullet	11 ,,
"Waste Last Pot"	6 ,,
Manganese	2½ oz.
Antimony	1 ,,
Gold (Precipitated)	5 drams.

"Very good pot as ever was made. Beautiful colour. Put colour in the middle of the pot."

ANOTHER RUBY.

Saltpetre	16 lb.
Sand	32 ,,
Red Lead	36 ,,
Manganese	1¾ oz.
Antimony	2 ,,
Gold (Precipitated)	1 ,,

"This mixture turned immediately it was put into the lear. Fill the pot for ruby a little at a time, and watch that it does not ferment. It does not require above twenty hours to fine; and mind the pot does not get too hot. When it is worked into lumps, put it into the lear with some fine ashes. Keep it turned often, and when a dark ruby get it down the lear; if it be not all dark, it will right itself in the plating. The metal from the pot should be a light straw colour."

A RUBY FROM COPPER.

	Cwt.	qrs.	lb.
Sand	4	2	0
Pearl Ashes	1	0	24
Red Lead	0	3	16
Carbonate of Lime	0	0	25
Phosphate of Lime	0	0	5
Red Tartar (Crude Tartar)	0	0	5
Borax	0	0	5
Oxide of Tin	0	0	$3\frac{1}{2}$
Red Oxide of Copper	0	0	$2\frac{1}{2}$

"Give it all the air you can, compatible with getting it plain; too great heat is against it."

FLINT FOR USING WITH THE RUBY FOR COATING (on pages 2 and 3).

Sand	64 lb.
Lead	72 ,,
Saltpetre	32 ,,
Manganese	1¼ oz.

"Charge your pot with two-thirds and 'dragade' it; next morning charge again with the rest and the ladings, and add 4 oz. manganese and 8 oz. of antimony."

A GERMAN METAL (Flint).

	Cwt.	qrs.	lb.
French Sand	10	0	0
Refined Soda	1	2	0
Common Soda Ash	3	2	0
Lime Spar	1	0	0
Fluor Spar	0	2	0
Nitrate of Soda	1	0	0

"Sand unburnt and unwashed. This mixture is given to form th· body of some of the following coloured metals, and is called 'German cullet or body'. These delicate colours require great care."

CORNELIAN, OR ALABASTER.

German Cullet (page 6)	35 lb.
Black Ash	15 oz.
Nitrate of Soda	8 ,,
Manganese	1 ,,

"This way very good."

ANOTHER CORNELIAN.

	Cwt.	qrs.	lb.	oz.
German Cullet (page 6)	4	1	0	0
Black Ash	0	0	11	0
Nitrate of Soda	0	0	7	0
Manganese	0	0	0	15

"Very good."

SAPPHIRE BLUE.

German Cullet (page 6)	14 lb.
Black Ash	5½ ,,
Nitrate of Soda	3½ ,,
Copper Scales	2 oz.

"Very good."

ANOTHER SAPPHIRE BLUE.

	Cwt.	qrs.	lb.
German Cullet (page 6)	3	1	0
Black Ash	0	0	11
Nitrate of Soda	0	0	8
Copper Scales	0	0	3¼
Blue Cullet	1	0	0

"Filled an overtaker. Very good."

ANOTHER SAPPHIRE BLUE.

	Cwt.	qrs.	lb.
German Cullet (page 6)	2	3	0
Cullet	1	2	0
Nitrate of Soda	0	0	7
Copper Scales	0	0	2½

"Very good."

CRYSOPHIS.

	Lb.	oz.	drs.
German Cullet (page 6) -	14	0	0
Black Ash - - - -	0	5½	0
Nitrate of Soda - - -	0	3½	0
Uranium (Oxide) - -	0	2	0
Green Oxide of Chrome -	0	0½	8
Sulphide of Copper - -	0	0	3

"Very good."

ANOTHER CRYSOPHIS.

	Cwt.	qrs.	lb.	oz.
German Cullet (page 6)	2	2	0	0
Crysophis Cullet - -	1	3	0	0
Saltpetre - - -	0	0	11	0
Oxide Uranium - -	0	0	2½	0
Sulphate of Copper	0	0	0	10

"Very good."

OPAL.

	Cwt.	qrs.	lb.	oz.
Sand	2	0	0	0
Lead	0	3	0	0
Ash	0	2	0	3
Plaster of Paris	0	2	0	0
Lime Spar	0	0	14	0
Manganese	0	0	0	3
Nitrate of Soda	0	0	7	0
Arsenic	0	0	0	8

ANOTHER OPAL.

	Cwt.	qrs.	lb.	oz.
Sand	2	2	0	0
Lead	1	1	0	0
Ash	1	0	11	0
Fluor Spar	0	1	24	0
Felspar	0	1	24	0
Saltpetre	0	0	12	0
Manganese	0	0	0	5

"Very good."

ANOTHER OPAL.

Sand	100 lb.
Lead	80 ,,
Ash	28 ,,
Saltpetre	30 ,,
Calcined Bones	20 ,,
Antimony	4 oz.

ANOTHER OPAL.

	Cwt.	qrs.	lb.	oz.
Sand	3	3	12	0
Cryolite	0	3	16	0
Lead	0	1	5	0
Soda	0	3	16	0
Nitrate of Soda	0	0	13	0
Arsenic	0	0	2	0
Manganese	0	0	0	3

"BEST" OPAL.

Sand	600 lb.
Soda	240 ,,
Felspar	225 ,,
Fluor Spar	225 ,,
Arsenic	6 ,,
Cryolite	5 ,,
Nitrate of Soda	65 ,,

ANOTHER OPAL.

	Cwt.	qrs.	lb.	oz.
Sand	1	3	20	0
Cryolite	0	1	22	0
Ash	0	0	20	0
Red Lead	0	0	20	0
Soda	0	1	22	0
Nitrate of Soda	0	0	8	0
Arsenic	0	0	1	0
Manganese	0	0	0	$1\frac{1}{2}$

ANOTHER OPAL.

	Cwt.	qrs.	lb.	oz.
French Sand	6	1	0	0
Lead	4	0	22	0
Ash (Pot)	3	1	6	0
Fluor Spar	1	1	12	0
Felspar	1	1	12	0
Saltpetre	0	1	8	0
Manganese	0	0	0	14

ANOTHER OPAL.

Sand	150 lb.
Soda	60 ,,
Nitrate of Soda	5 ,,
Barytes	13 ,,
Arsenic	8 oz.
Manganese	5 ,,

"This was changed into blue by adding oxide of cobalt, 4 oz., and about 40 lb. of blue cullet."

ANOTHER OPAL.

Sand	700 lb.
Red Lead	470 ,,
Ash (Marshall's)	370 ,,
Felspar	152 ,,
Fluor Spar	152 ,,
Saltpetre	36 ,,
Manganese	14 oz.

ANOTHER OPAL.*

Sand	600 lb.
Soda (B., M. & Co.)	240 ,,
Felspar	225 ,,
Fluor Spar	225 ,,
Arsenic	6 ,,
Cryolite	5 ,,
Nitrate of Soda	65 ,,

TURQUOISE BLUE.

Sand	100 lb.
Red Lead	80 ,,
Saltpetre	28 ,,
Ash	28 ,,
Calcined Bones	18 ,,
Arsenic	4 ,,
Brass Filings	1½ ,,

ANOTHER TURQUOISE.

	Cwt.	qrs.	lb.
Batch	0	1	12
Turquoise Cullet	3	0	0
Oxide of Iron	0	0	1
Copper Scales	0	0	2
Opal Cullet	0	1	12

"Very good, very soft, not regular batch; work immediately it is fine; last instruction important."

ANOTHER TURQUOISE.

Batch (A, page 22)	504 parts.
Plaster of Paris	14 ,,
Fluor Spar	24 ,,
Felspar	24 ,,
Arsenic	6 ,,
Black Oxide of Copper	9 ,,
Black Oxide of Cobalt	$2\frac{3}{4}$ oz.
Phosphate of Lime	9 parts.

ANOTHER TURQUOISE.

Opal Batch (* page 13)	28 lb.
Arsenic	4 oz.
Zaffer	$1\frac{1}{2}$,,
Brass	12 ,,
Cullet (Turquoise)	70 lb.

GOLD COLOUR.

	Cwt.	qrs.	lb.
Sand - - - - -	1	1	0
Soda - - - - -	0	2	4
Spar - - - - -	0	0	25
Calcined Oats - - -	0	0	1

"Good and right."

ANOTHER GOLD COLOUR.

	Cwt.	qrs.	lb.
Amber Cullet - - -	3	0	0
Batch (A, page 22) - -	0	3	0
Calcined Oats - - -	0	0	¾

"Very good. You may calcine your own oats in the lear or furnace. Sometimes ground and sifted coke is used, but it is not so pure a carbon."

DARK GREEN.

Cullet	112 lb.
Batch (A, page 22)	336 ,,
Crocus Marcus	13 ,,
Copper Scales	4 ,,
Oxide of Copper	3 oz.

" Very good."

ANOTHER GREEN (Common).

	Cwt.	qrs.	lb.	oz.
Green Cullet	1	0	0	0
Batch (A, page 22)	0	2	24	0
Oxide of Iron	0	0	4	0
Copper Scales	0	0	1	0
Oxide of Copper	0	0	0	1

GREEN FOR MALACHITE.

	Cwt.	qrs.	lb.	oz.
Green Cullet	1	0	0	0
Green Siftings	0	3	0	0
Batch (A, page 22)	0	2	24	0
Oxide of Iron	0	0	4	0
Copper Scales	0	0	1	0
Oxide of Copper	0	0	0	2

" Very good."

BLUE FOR MALACHITE.

	Cwt.	qrs.	lb.	oz.
Batch (A, page 22)	3	2	0	0
Blue Cullet	1	0	0	0
Zaffer	0	0	5	0
Manganese	0	0	0	8

BLACK FOR MALACHITE.

Use Batch A, page 22, and treat it as Crystal Batch on page 19, and this will produce a black metal which will incorporate with the blue and green metal above, and will anneal safely.

"These three colours will work mixed from the pots; one gathered upon the other and manipulated on the 'marver,' then pressed, or melted in again in the furnace and blown; anneal them well."

BLACK.

Batch (Crystal Batch)	56 lb.
Flint Cullet	56 ,,
Manganese	12 ,,
Iron Scales	3 ,,

"A good pot of black which was not greasy."

COMMON CANARY BATCH.

Sand	1,100 lb.
Ash	336 ,,
Spar	264 ,,
Lead	100 ,,
Nitrate of Soda	40 ,,
Arsenic	6 ,,
Oxide Uranium	$4\frac{1}{2}$,,

CANARY.

Batch (as above)	14 lb.
Uranium	1 oz.
Sulphate of Copper	$\frac{3}{4}$,,

"This gives the proportion of colourings to 14 lb. batch."

ANOTHER CANARY.

Batch (as above)	336 lb.
Canary Cullet	100 ,,
Oxide Uranium	14 oz.

WHITE OPAQUE GLASS.

Sand	100 parts.
Calcined Ash	50 ,,
Slacked Lime	16 ,,
Oxide of Tin	60 ,,

ANOTHER WHITE OPAQUE GLASS.

Sand	100 parts.
Minium	78 ,,
Calcined Ash	30 ,,
Nitrate of Soda (Crystals)	8 ,,
White Oxide of Tin	62 ,,

"These will be interesting, as they are from a very old book of recipes."

SEALING WAX—RED—(Experiment).

Saltpetre	3 lb.
Lead	6 ,,
Sand	9 ,,
"Raw Brass"	1 ,,
"Colclother of Vitriol"	1 ,,
Red Tartar	1 ,,

"Was a wax red, but faded. Wanted working when plain, probably."

ANOTHER WAX—RED.

Cullet (out of the above experiment)	20 lb.
Added—Red Tartar	2 ,,
Brass	8 oz.
Colcothar of Vitriol	1 lb.

"This produced a good wax red after being in the furnace twelve hours. The colour was throughout very good."

FLINT (A)—(A very cheap Metal).

	Cwt.	qrs.	lb.	oz.
Sand - - - -	12	2	0	0
Alkali (B., M. & Co.) -	4	1	0	0
Ash (Marshall's) - -	0	3	18	0
Spar - - - -	1	0	8	0
Barytes - - -	0	3	14	0
Nitrate of Soda - -	0	2	18	0
Arsenic - - -	0	0	5	0
Manganese (about) -	0	0	1	14

"Costs about 2s. 8d. per cwt. into pot. (Evaporation 13 to 15 per cent.)"

A BATCH (B)—(A little more costly).

	Cwt.	qrs.	lb.
Sand - - - - -	12	0	0
Soda (B., M. & Co.) - -	4	1	0
Lead - - - - -	0	1	0
Spar - - - - -	1	0	0
Nitrate of Soda - - -	0	2	0
Saltpetre - - - -	0	2	0
Arsenic - - - -	0	0	2
Manganese - - - -	0	0	$1\frac{1}{4}$

"Costs about 3s. 2d. per cwt."

FLINT GLASS (Crystal and Demi).*

Refined Pearl Ashes	76 lb.
Saltpetre	10 ,,
Lead	200 ,,
Sand	260 ,,
Manganese	4 drs.
Arsenic	8 lb.

* Nearly every house in Britain uses different proportions, but we give a variety. The costs will be apparent to the mixer.

ANOTHER CRYSTAL FLINT GLASS.

	Best.	Common.
Sand	560 lb.	500 lb.
Lead	330 ,,	350 ,,
Ash	160 ,,	150 ,,
Saltpetre	60 ,,	30 ,,
Arsenic	1 ,,	1 ,,

ANOTHER CRYSTAL FLINT GLASS.

Sand	520 lb.
Lead	360 ,,
Ash	160 ,,
Saltpetre	35 ,,

"Colouring."

ANOTHER FLINT (C).

	Cwt.	qrs.	lb.	oz.
Sand	12	2	0	0
Alkali (B., M. & Co.)	4	1	0	0
Ash (Marshall's)	0	3	18	0
Spar	1	0	8	0
Barytes	0	3	14	0
Nitrate of Soda	0	2	18	0
Arsenic	0	0	5	0
Manganese	0	0	1	14

"Costs about 3s. 7¼d. per cwt. Very good. Evaporation 13 to 15 per cent."

ANOTHER FLINT (D).

	Cwt.	qrs.	lb.
Sand	12	0	0
Soda (B., M. & Co.)	4	0	0
Nitrate of Soda	1	0	0
Ash	0	1	0
Lead	0	1	0
Spar	1	0	0
Arsenic	0	0	7
Manganese	0	0	1

"Costs about 2s. 10d. per cwt. Evaporation 13 to 15 per cent."

FLINT (a good blowing Metal).

	Cwt.	qrs.	lb.
Sand - - - - -	12	0	0
Alkali - - - -	4	0	0
Lead - - - - -	1	0	0
Saltpetre - - - -	1	0	0
Spar - - - - -	1	0	0
Ash - - - - -	0	2	0
Arsenic - - - -	0	0	5
Manganese - - -	0	0	2
Cobalt - - - -	11 grs.		

"Costs about 4s. 6d. per cwt."

ACHROMATIC GLASS.

Lead	500 lb.
Sand	600 ,,
Ashes (Refined)	180 ,,
Saltpetre	60 ,,
Manganese	7 oz.
Antimony	3 ,,

"This is the right quantity."

PASTE GLASS.

Furnace let out, and pots allowed to cool.

Refined Pearl Ashes	97 parts.
Lead	200 ,,
Sand	260 ,,
Saltpetre	10 ,,
Manganese	$\tfrac{1}{2}$ oz.
Arsenic	12 ,,

"The paste was very good. The foundering was kept twenty-four hours longer, but the furnace was kept little hotter than a working furnace, and was then let out gradually, being kept for twelve hours little better than a pot arch. This paste was perfect to the bottom of the pot when broken up."

WHITE ENAMEL.

Sand	50 lb.
Saltpetre	20 ,,
Lead	50 ,,
Arsenic	4½ ,,
Antimony	½ ,,

"A very good pot of white, and worked clear."

FIRESTONE.

Sand	125 lb.
Saltpetre	30 ,,
Lead	150 ,,
Arsenic	7½ ,,
Antimony	½ ,

"This was a pot of very good firestone."

DEAD WHITE (for Moons).

Sand	28 lb.
Lead	21 ,,
Ashes	11 ,,
Arsenic	2½ oz.
White Cullet	200 lb.

"A very good pot. Worked clear and well."

WHITE AGATE.

Sand	24 lb.
Lead	25 ,,
Saltpetre	15 ,,
Calcined Bone Ash	1 ,,
Arsenic	4 ,,

ANOTHER AGATE.

Sand	67 lb.
Lead	54 ,,
Ash	20 ,,
Saltpetre	11 ,,
Arsenic	6 ,,
Bone Ash	10 ,,

"Very good."

CANARY.

Sand	$5\frac{1}{4}$ parts.
Lead	$3\frac{1}{2}$,,
Ash	$1\frac{1}{8}$,,
Saltpetre	$\frac{1}{2}$,,
Oxide Uranium	$\frac{1}{358}$,,

"No arsenic. No manganese. Well mixed in a clean harbour. As a rule it takes 5 oz. of uranium to the cwt. Don't use the blacks from the iron when you use the cullet. This is a very tender colour to make."

CANARY ENAMEL.

To Blacks (Cullet)	100 lb.
Use Chromate of Lead	$\frac{3}{4}$,,

"Dissolve any quantity of lead (sugar of lead) in warm water; dissolve chromate of potash in warm water; put the one into the other by degrees, stirring all the while with a glass rod till no more precipitate falls; strain off the liquid and wash the precipitate which is chromate of lead; filter it, and it is fit for use. Don't use the chromate of lead of commerce; it is not pure."

INDEX.

ACHROMATIC glass, 26.
Agate, white, 28.
Alabaster, 7.

"BEST" opal, 11.
Black, 19.
Black for malachite, 18.
Blue for malachite, 18.
Blue, sapphire, 8.
Blue, turquoise, 14, 15.

CANARY, 19, 29.
Canary batch, common, 19.
Canary enamel, 29.
Common canary batch, 19.
Common green, 17.
Cornelian, 7.
Crysophis, 9.
Crystal flint glass, 23.

DARK green, 17.
Dead white (for moons), 28.

ENAMEL, canary, 29.
Enamel, white, 27.

FIRESTONE, 27.
Flint, 22, 23, 24, 25.
Flint for using with the ruby for coating (on pages 2 and 3), 5.

GERMAN metal, A (flint), 6.

Glass, achromatic, 26.
Glass, flint (crystal and demi), 22, 23, 24, 25.
Glass, paste, 26.
Gold colour, 16.
Green, common, 17.
Green, dark, 17.
Green for malachite, 18.

MALACHITE, black for, 18.
Malachite, blue for, 18.
Malachite, green for, 18.

OPAL, 10, 11, 12, 13.
Opal, "Best," 11.
Opaque glass, white, 20.

PASTE glass, 26.

RED sealing wax, 21.
Ruby, 1, 2, 3.
Ruby from copper, 4.

SAPPHIRE blue, 8.
Sealing wax, red, 21.

TURQUOISE blue, 14, 15.

WHITE, agate, 28.
White, dead (for moons), 28.
White enamel, 27.
White opaque glass, 20.

www.ingramcontent.com/pod-product-compliance
Lightning Source LLC
Chambersburg PA
CBHW080433110426
42743CB00016B/3153